The ORIGIN
of NAMES,
WORDS and
EVERYTHING
in BETWEEN

VOLUME II

Published by Mango Publishing, a division of Mango Publishing Group,Inc.

Cover Design: Morgane Leoni
Art Direction: Morgane Leoni

For permission requests, please contact the publisher at:

Mango Publishing Group
2850 Douglas Road, 2nd Floor
Coral Gables, FL 33134 U.S.A.
info@mango.bz

For special orders, quantity sales, course adoptions and corporate sales, please email the publisher at sales@mango.bz. For trade and wholesale sales, please contact Ingram Publisher Services at: customer.service@ingramcontent.com or +1.800.509.4887.

The Origins of Names, Words, and Everything in Between: Volume II

Library of Congress Cataloging-in-Publication number: 2021942638
ISBN: (print) 978-1-64250-681-5, (ebook) 978-1-64250-682-2
BISAC category code: LAN024000 LANGUAGE ARTS & DISCIPLINES / Linguistics / Etymology

Printed in the United States of America.

The ORIGIN of NAMES, WORDS and EVERYTHING in BETWEEN

VOLUME II

Patrick Foote

mango
PUBLISHING GROUP

CORAL GABLES

CONTENTS

Hello Again!

Well, here we are again. For lack of a better term and at the risk of sounding a tad too cheesy, the adventure continues! I hope you are all just as excited as myself to look into the origins of more names, words, and everything in between. Looking back at that first book feels like the tip of the iceberg, and, believe me, this is quite a big iceberg. Simply due to the fact that these books are all about uncovering how things got their names. Luckily for name nerds like myself and for the etymologically excitable like yourself, everything has a name.

So it's time to dive back into the world of word origins yet again. Once again, I have found a plethora of names and words to share and explain to you all. Like last time, this book is split into themed sections, covering names that fit neatly into that section. From the most popular thing in that area, which you may have always wondered about, to how it got its name, to some lesser known but enjoyably named things. I'm sure you understand—this is the sequel, after all, and who reads the sequel book first?! You have read the first book, haven't you? Well, just in case there's anyone out there who is leaping into Volume II before reading Volume I, let's have a quick recap of things, shall we?

WHO AM I?

The name of the person who wrote this book all about names is Patrick Foote—that's me, by the way, not quite sure why I wrote that in the third person. I have been studying etymology and word origins for roughly five years or so now. Though I must admit, when I say "studying word origins," I don't mean studying them in some fancy library, at a well-respected university, or at some cushy educational job. I study word origins primarily in my basement or sometimes in a coffee shop if I'm starting to scratch at the walls. As I study word origins for my YouTube channel *Name Explain*, which is all about pretty much what it sounds like, explaining names.

The channel had pretty humble beginnings; it started as something to do when I wasn't stacking the shelves of a supermarket during my day job. As the channel grew, I had to take risks, from leaving university where I was studying words to leaving the supermarket that paid my bills to leaving my parents and their home, which had always been a safety net for me. Yet those risks paid off as *Name Explain* is now one of the most popular YouTube channels focusing on etymology. It has allowed me to make uncovering etymologies my full-time job and even given me the chance to write these books, something that I am eternally grateful for. So while I may not have the academic credentials or a degree in the field, and I never claim to be a professional by any means, I do have a burning passion for word origins and plenty of experience googling answers, so you're in safe hands. At least, I think so anyway.

WHAT IS ETYMOLOGY?

I have already used that big word a couple of times now, etymology. It's a word that came to us from the Greeks with their word *etymologia*, meaning "to find the true origins of a word." It's basically a fancy word for word origins. But it's one I love, so I'll be using it quite a lot in this book. Etymologies can come from a huge variety of places. As we just saw with the word etymology itself, words can come from ancient roots. Greek and Latin often play a large role, especially with the English language, so I have no doubts those languages will be popping up again in this book.

However, words can come to us through all kinds of etymologies. Some words are formed when we put other words together, like how the word *armchair* is just the words *arm* and *chair* put together. Sometimes, we use a whole string of words that become a mouthful to say every time, so we just take the first letter of each word and use that as a word unto itself. Like how the self-contained underwater breathing apparatus was shortened to just SCUBA. Sometimes words are named after people or places important to them, sometimes they have fun stories linked to them, and sometimes they are just made up out of thin air.

9

All etymologies are exciting in their own way, that's for sure. And while every word does have an etymology, sometimes, the passage of time, means, and lack of ancient information means we aren't exactly sure what that etymology is. The greatest struggle of any etymologist is that the spoken word can't be preserved like a dinosaur bone or an ancient piece of pottery. Some of the greatest unsolved mysteries we have still are the unknown origins of words. But that's incredible unto itself. Take the word *dog*; no one exactly knows where the word *dog* came from. Isn't it amazing that a word so commonplace as *dog* can also be equally mysterious?

WHAT ETYMOLOGIES ARE IN THIS BOOK?

As mentioned, Volume I was the tip of the iceberg. With that book, I wanted to cover the big picture, obvious topics. If you were to ask someone to name things that have names, it would have been the topics of Volume I: countries, animals, towns, objects, planets, etc. While I could have easily found more entries on those same topics for this volume, this time, I went for completely new topics. Topics and themes from a huge variety of different fields, which I am sure you are already aware of, as you've probably seen the contents page by now. There are some less obvious topics covered this time around, that's for sure, but of course, everything has a name, so anything is up for covering, no matter how niche it may seem.

I also wanted to somewhat look at the other side of the coin in regard to the various subjects I covered last time. In Volume I, we looked at countries and cities on our planet today; this time around, we look into former, historic places that used to be on our globe. And we shone a huge spotlight on the animal kingdom last time around, so this time, let's shine a light on the plant kingdom instead and give the planet's greenery the recognition it deserves. I still do cover some pretty obvious stuff in this book too. How did I fail to talk about bodies of water in the last book? And colours for that matter? Though perhaps most shocking is that in the last book,

I failed to properly talk about the most commonplace names on our planet. The names of us! We all have names, and it's these first names I want to talk about first.

11

First Names

First name, given name, Christian name, whatever you want to call it. It's something pretty much all of us have. They are something that come to define us; your first name is pretty much you. When people think of names, it's most likely these kinds of names that come to mind first. What's also great with first names is that they all have a meaning, some of those not as great as others. The names I have chosen here were picked for a variety of reasons. I wanted to uncover the origins of some of the world's most popular names, reveal some odd meanings for other popular names, and share with you all some names from around the world you may not have heard of before. Anyway, let's have some fun with first names!

OLIVER

In many parts of the world, especially in English-speaking countries, Oliver is one of the most popular boy names there is, so it only seemed fitting to start things off with perhaps the most popular name. Despite being such a popular name at the moment, we don't have one definitive idea as to where the name came from. Most sources agree that it came to England with the Normans in 1066 as the Norman name *Olivier,* but as to how the Normans got that name, we have a couple of ideas. One idea is that it came from Latin and their word *oliva,* which fittingly means olive tree. The Romans *loved* olives—of course, they are tasty, but the Romans and other residents of the ancient Mediterranean saw them as more than just a delicious snack. The olive and its tree came to be a symbol of peace; we still use the term "extend the olive branch" today when we are seeking peace with someone. It makes all the sense in the world that a fruit this beloved would create a first name.

Another theory for its origin isn't quite as fruity. It's also thought that the Norman name *Olivier* came from the Middle Low German name *Alfihar*, which means things along the lines of elf-host or even elf-army. The idea of hosting elves sounds pretty cool to me, and the idea of having an army of elves sounds even cooler, though maybe that's just me being too much of a geek. Nevertheless, either the Latin *oliva* or the Middle Low German *Alfihar* went on to become the Norman *Olivier*, which was brought to England where it became Oliver and would eventually take the baby-naming world by storm.

MALLORY

While certainly a pretty-sounding name, which garnered it a spike in popularity in the 1980s, its meaning is not as pretty. In fact, this name is rather unfortunate, quite literally. No, seriously, the name "Mallory" means exactly that: unfortunate. Once again, this is a name of French origins, coming from the old name of *Malheure*, meaning unfortunate or unlucky. The real question here is why would we create a name with such an unenjoyable meaning to begin with?

Well, to understand that we have to understand how we created names as a whole to begin with—pretty big concept stuff for only entry two, I know. Lots of first names started life as surnames; however, surnames became a thing after first names; to begin with, we all just had one name. As places got more populated, many people would have the same first name, meaning extra names were needed to help differentiate people. People started adding extra names to the end of their first names to help them stand out. These second names became known as bynames, basically just old nicknames; these bynames could be inspired by where they lived or what they did for work, just to name a few examples. Eventually, people started to take great pride in their bynames and passed them on to their children, hence how we created the modern concept of a surname!

So how does Mallory fit into all this? Well, as well as being inspired by jobs and homes, bynames could also be inspired by the characteristics of the people who had them. It must have been the case that the French byname of *Malheure* was given to some unlucky and unfortunate people. As a byname for the downtrodden, it became an inherited surname and then became the first name Mallory as we know it today. What's great is that despite this gloomy meaning, it hasn't stopped people from choosing the name after all these years.

CALVIN

Calvin is yet another name that doesn't have the greatest of meanings. Calvin has similar roots to Mallory. It too started out as a name given to people due to a characteristic of the holder of the name. Yet, instead of being a metaphysical characteristic like being unfortunate, it was a physical characteristic that inspired it. Calvin dates all the way to Ancient Rome with the cognomen of *Calvinus*. A "cognomen" is pretty much the Ancient Roman equivalent of the bynames we talked about earlier, in which someone would be honoured with an additional name that reflected them personally. So what did the cognomen of *Calvinus* mean? Well, it meant bald, as in not having any hair upon your head. So when this name made its way into English as the first name Calvin, it still meant bald.

Okay, so maybe I am being too harsh on the name Calvin. There's honestly nothing wrong with being bald; it's a natural thing. Yet, human society has made balding a laughing matter, so much so that when I read that a first name means bald, I can't help but find it funny. I'll try my best not to be as "baldist" in the future. Apologies to any Calvins or bald people reading this book right now. Though this also explains to us why, in Spanish, the word for bald is *calvo*, as Spanish is a language that relates deeply to Latin.

JESSICA

We all know the classic story about the name Jessica; it was a name created by The Bard himself, William Shakespeare. Well, while Will did do an awful lot for the English language (and yes, the earliest source we have for the name does come from his play *The Merchant of Venice*), to declare that he created the name Jessica out of thin air isn't quite the case.

The popular idea is that Shakespeare molded the name Jessica from an ancient, already existing name. That name being the ancient Biblical name of *Iscah*, which itself derives from the Hebrew roots of *Yiskah*. The name wasn't too prevalent in the pages of the Bible; most noticeably, it belonged to a niece of Abraham. It means "to behold," and when The Bard stumbled upon this name, he must have liked it so much that he retooled it into the name Jessica, and, to this day, Jessica is still seen as having the meaning "to behold."

While on the subject of names "created" by Shakespeare, other names he lays claim to are Olivia, Miranda, Perdita, Florizel, Imogen, and Othello. But like with the name Jessica, he didn't create these names out of thin air but crafted them from words and names already established in the language.

ALEXANDER

This is a name held by some of the greatest figures in history, from the inventor of the telephone Alexander Graham Bell to founding US father Alexander Hamilton. The name, however, started life as a nickname for one specific person. That being the legendary Greek figure of Paris, whose name has nothing to do with the city, in case you were wondering. Paris' most notable story from Greek mythology is when he eloped with Helen of Troy, which sparked the famous Trojan War. However, as a young man, he helped many and defended those who needed help. In one instance, he helped some shepherds whose flock of sheep were being stolen. The shepherds thanked him for his help and gave him the title of *Aléxandros*.

This title comes from two Greek words, *alexein*, which means "to defend/ward off," and *anēr*, which means "man." So this title is seen as meaning "defending men/defender of men," which is a pretty darn heroic meaning if I do say so myself. Of course, this name would go on to become a first name and morph into Alexander. It would also eventually be given to someone even more heroic than Paris of the Greek myths, that being Alexander the III of Macedon, more known by his title of Alexander the Great. As king of the ancient kingdom of Macedonia, he won countless wars and claimed huge amounts of land. As a great war leader, it was only fitting he too bear this name Alexander, which means "defender of man."

LAKEISHA

African American culture has a rich history with inventive first names, and Lakeisha is a prime example of this. African American names have drawn inspiration from a huge variety of sources, whether that be from the continent of Africa or the United States. Another large influence on African American names is the French language, as France in the past laid claims to various parts of the Americas, such as the area that now makes up the state of Louisiana or the land that makes up the modern nation of Haiti. Both these areas still have a variation of French spoken in them. These areas would have been populated with African Americans too, so the French language impacted them and their names. The

La at the start of the name Lakeisha comes from French roots; in French, it simply means "the," and we see French prefixes in a few African American names, like with Demarcus or Lebron.

What about the Keisha part then? Well, there seem to be two main theories as to where this part of the name comes from. One idea is that it comes from African roots meaning "favourite;" however, I find it odd that most sources that say this don't specify an exact African language because obviously Africa isn't just one single nation where they all speak the same tongue. The idea with more evidence is that it comes from the Hebrew name of *Keziah*, which means "cinnamon." This might sound odd, but remember, cinnamon comes from a tree and, as we established with Oliver, it's not a weird thing to name people after trees.

Before we continue, I must stress that while I have been calling this an African American name, that doesn't mean it has only been used by African American people. Lakeisha (like many other names) is undoubtedly a creation of Black Americans, though it's used far and wide.

MUHAMMAD

Many argue that Muhammad is the most popular name in the world; that's kind of true and not true. While it is popular, and many do have the name, it's not the number-one name in a lot of nations. The primary reason this is the case is because there are quite a few spelling variations of the name, including Mohammed, Mohammad, Mihammad, and Muhamad, just to name a few examples. When we include all these different spelling variations, then Muhammad does quite possibly become the world's most popular name. Though none of these individual spellings of the name lay claim as the world's most popular.

Regardless of whether it's number one in the world or not, you can't argue that it is a darn popular name. The reason behind its popularity is the religion of Islam. The prophet of Islam has this name too. This means that many Muslim parents choose to give their sons the same name as their prophet, as he is seen as the embodiment of excellence, and it's hoped that by sharing the prophet's name, they too will lead a life like the prophet Muhammad. As for where the name comes from, however, it's thought to derive from the Arabic verb of *hamida*, which means "to praise," so in turn, the name Muhammad is seen as meaning things like "praised," "praiseworthy," and even "commendable." It's fitting that someone so praised and beloved by so many people around the world has a name meaning just that.

HINA

This simple name has become common in a few Asian languages. It is most noticeable, however, as a Japanese female name. As this name is Japanese, it means that it's not usually spelt with the Latin alphabet of English and other Latin-based languages. More often than not, it is spelt with Kanji, characters that represent entire words or phrases, unlike the characters of our alphabet that represent individual sounds. The name Hina isn't created from just one or two sets of Kanji characters, however; one source points out that the name Hina can be created in Japanese through over one hundred different Kanji combinations and variations! That also means that all these different Kanji combos that create the name Hina give it different meanings too.

The most popular idea is that the name Hina means "light/sunshine." Though others claim the name means "male" (which is odd considering it's primarily a girl's name) or that it means "vegetation." A troubling thing with Kanji is that those symbols can be interpreted to mean a variety of different things. Nevertheless, Hina is a pretty-sounding name, regardless of what Kanji characters you spell it with.

SANTIAGO

As well as being a first name across the Spanish- and Portuguese-speaking world, Santiago is also a surname and a place name. There are many settlements with this name, including the capital of Chile! This is also a name that comes from religious origins. The first part of this name is pretty easy to understand; it comes from the Spanish *santo* and means "saint." As I said, it is a religious name. So yes, this name comes from a saint of Christianity, and what I like about this name is that despite the fact that these saints already have first names, which kids could be named after, their title of saint is being used as an actual first name.

21

Though what saint specifically does the name Santiago relate to? Saint Iago? Well, kind of. The latter part of this name comes from the name *Yago*, which is an old Spanish form of the name James. So Santiago is a name that means Saint James. As I mentioned, why not just call your kid James if you want to name them after the saint? Though not only did Saint James give us the name of Santiago, but also the name Santiago eventually got shortened into its own name entirely, Diego! Well, that's one theory as to how the name Diego came about, anyway.

WANGARI

Kenya is home to the Kikuyu people, who make up roughly 17 percent of the entire Kenyan population. This name of Wangari is a girl's name from the Kikuyu language. It is thought to come from their word *ngarĩ*, which means "leopard" in their tongue. Leopards are pretty cool animals to be named after, that's for sure. Especially considering that animal-based names aren't all too common in the English-speaking world. The name Wangari itself is best known to the Kikuyu people in their creation myth. One of the nine daughters of their creation goddess Mumbi was named Wangari. Mumbi is also used as a girl's name in Kikuyu, meaning "she who creates" or "she who builds," which are pretty cool but not quite as cool as being named after a leopard in my eyes.

Historic Places

The world as we know it today hasn't always been this way. Our blue ball has been floating in space and has changed dramatically over the years. Borders that once existed on maps have been erased and redrawn; grand cities that once stood are now rubble; and even the land we walk on has split apart, merged, and moved across the planet. In Volume I, we spent a good amount of time looking into the names of places on our planet; this time around, I want to step back in time and marvel upon the historical places on our planet that are no longer here, or at least don't exist in the same way they did at the peak of their power. The names I have chosen here include former countries, cities, regions, and empires ranging from the not-too-distant past all the way back to before we humans were even here.

MESOPOTAMIA

This is quite possibly the most important place in human history. Often known as the "Cradle of Civilization," Mesopotamia is where we humans stopped being hunter-gatherers and started forming societies like the ones we know today. The wheel, math, and writing are all inventions of those who lived in Mesopotamia. Life was able to kickstart in such a way here due to a variety of factors, including the fertility of the soil in the area and the climate. Parts of the modern nations of Iraq, Iran, Kuwait, Syria, and Turkey in Western Asia on the cusp of the Arabian Peninsula are where Mesopotamians resided.

Mesopotamia wasn't a single kingdom or nation, but rather the name for the land various tribes and people thrived in, such as the Babylonians and Sumerians. They for sure didn't call the land Mesopotamia either. It's a name given to the land retroactively by the Greeks, so it's of Greek origin. As mentioned, the people of ancient Mesopotamia could thrive because the soil there was so darn fertile, meaning farming could be achieved. The reason this soil was so good to farm on was because Mesopotamia resided between two rivers that enhanced the soil there—these two rivers being the Tigris and Euphrates. Its position in the middle of two rivers is why it now has the name Mesopotamia, as this name comes from the Greek words of *meso*, which means "middle," and *potamos*, meaning "river," so the name simply means "land in the middle of rivers." This Greek *meso* is seen in names of other parts of the world too, like the name Mesoamerica which we use for the land in the centre of the continent of the Americas.

25

YUGOSLAVIA

This nation existed twice on our planet, first from 1918 till 1941, and then again from 1945 all the way till 1992. It's intentional that those dates line up with the World Wars, as Yugoslavia was officially created in the immediate aftermath of the First World War. During the Second World War, it was claimed and split up by the Axis powers, only for it to reemerge at the end of the war. The nation lasted all the way until the early 1990s, and in its place today lie the nations of Slovenia, Croatia, Bosnia and Herzegovina, Serbia, Montenegro, Kosovo, and North

Macedonia. What connects all these nations? (Well, minus once all being one large nation, of course.) It's their language and their people, all being South Slavic. While the nation only existed in the twentieth century, the idea of one large country containing all the South Slavic people dates back hundreds of years. This should explain to us where the *Slavia* part of the name comes from. That ever-present -ia suffix means "land of the," so this can be seen as meaning "land of the Slavs."

Why *Yugo*, however? These four letters don't appear in any of the names of the nations that now exist, so where did it come from? Well, remember I mentioned Yugoslavia was specifically for Southern Slavs? This *Yugo* part relates to their southerly location. It's worth mentioning here that South Slavic is different from North Slavic; North Slavic (which is often split into East and West Slavic) includes the likes of Russian, Polish, and Czech. Anyway, Yugo comes from the Old Church Slavonic *jugu*, which means "south." Combining this with the aforementioned Slavia shows us that the name as a whole means "land of the Southern Slavs," which is fitting as that was exactly what this country was.

PRUSSIA

Prussia was a kingdom within the German Empire. A kingdom within an empire, that's some pretty impressive stuff right there. While the German Empire started life in 1871, the Kingdom of Prussia outdated the empire that would consume it, being formed in 1701. However, both the German Empire and the Kingdom of Prussia would cease to be in 1918, once again in the aftermath of the First World War. What was once Prussia doesn't neatly fit into a modern country or two, but instead, parts of former Prussia now reside in parts of Denmark, Germany, Belgium, Czechia, Poland, Russia, and Lithuania.

The name of Prussia is believed to derive from a tribe of people who once lived in the land that Prussia once resided in, especially the area approximately around the Baltic Sea. These people are known as either the Old Prussians, *Prūsai,* or *Prusi.* Where their name came from, however, we don't seem to be sure. Ideas link it possible to geographic roots relating to the many bodies of water in this region of the world. Though once Germanic people rocked up and took over this land, they clearly liked the name enough to keep it.

Now, I am aware of how much this name sounds like Russia; it's still a debated topic as to whether these names are linked or not. A lot of people seem to chalk it up to coincidence, as we seemingly know that Russia was named after the Rus people. Though these Rus people did live in close proximity to the Old Prussians, so perhaps there was some intermixing. One idea even claims that the name Prussia comes from the old Slavic *po-rus,* which means "land near the Rus," so maybe these names are more connected than we thought.

SPARTA

We all have an image of ancient Greece in our head: the robes, buildings lined with columns, gods, and monsters ruling over all of us. Yet, despite this, ancient Greece wasn't a singular place. It's not like it's just the modern nation of Greece but a few thousand years ago. At the time of ancient Greece, which is thought to be from around the twelfth century BC to around 600 AD, it wasn't just one country. Instead, the land of ancient Greece was split between small city-states. Each of these cities ruled themselves, and they didn't all get along at the best of times. Some of these city-states include Athens (which is still the nation's capital), Corinth, Olympia, and perhaps the most well-known of them all, Sparta.

The city-state of Sparta is best known for its military might, fearsome soldiers, and their blunt, to-the-point way of speaking. Spartan boys started training at the age of seven, and qualities such as discipline and endurance were drilled into them. We all know the story of the three hundred Spartans and their battles against the Persians. War and battles were the top priorities of the Spartans, and their city-state lasted from the 900s BC to 192 BC.

While we know a lot about their battles, as to where their name comes from, we aren't too sure. There are a few ideas I dug up in regards to its origin. One idea has it relating to ancient words meaning to sow/spread, as the land in the city was fertile; this etymology ties the name Sparta into the adjective of sparse, which means scattered. While another idea is that it came from the Greek *sparte*, meaning a "type of cord," it's thought that maybe this cord was used to define the city's boundaries. Ancient writer Homer called Sparta "the country of beautiful women," though I think that was more his personal idea than its actual etymology.

The Spartans and ancient Greeks, however, only called the precise city Sparta; we use that name for the surrounding area as a whole now. They called the land where Sparta was a whole *Lacedaemon/Laconia*. While we don't know where this name came from exactly, what we do know is that it created the adjective of laconic, which means to speak in a blunt way, much like the blunt precise language the Spartans themselves used.

MANCHUKUO

Once upon a time, this country resided in an area that now makes up a part of modern-day China. It existed in one form or another from 1932 to 1945 and was a puppet state. What's a puppet state? Well, without this book diving too much into the nitty-gritty of politics and empires, a puppet state is a nation that is officially independent but behind the scenes being controlled by a higher power. The higher power in this case being the Kingdom of Japan. Japan formed this puppet state as something of a distraction, to divert eyes away from their other actions and to formally lay claim to land in what is now northeastern China.

29

This area of the world already somewhat bears this name. Manchuria is the English language name for this northeast corner of Asia, which now homes part of China and Russia. The name for this area derives from the Manchu people who live in the area. Their name is thought to mean "strong arrow" by some scholars, perhaps in relation to their weapon of choice. How we got Manchukuo is kind of long winded. In Japanese, the land was called *Manshūkoku*, which, in Mandarin, was pronounced Mǎnzhōuguó, and then this Mandarin name was romanised (which means to put a word into the Latin alphabet) into Manchukuo as we know it.

BOHEMIA

The historic region of Bohemia now makes up the western half of the nation of Czechia. Throughout its existence, Bohemia was its own independent principality and parts of other empires like the Holy Roman Empire and the Austro-Hungarian Empire. Bohemia, like many other places, was named after the tribe that initially settled the land. They were a Celtic tribe named the Boii, and where their name came from, we aren't too sure. It's thought to either relate to cows or warriors, so it's believed these people were either named after their fighting abilities or their herding abilities. I guess these things are kind of similar.

What's most interesting about Bohemia is its legacy on language to this day. The land of Bohemia created the adjective of bohemian. What does bohemian describe? Well, yes, while it can describe things from Bohemia, it also describes people, places, and things that are unconventional, free-spirited, and creative. It's used especially in the world of arts; poets and painters are known to be bohemian, or boho as it has been shortened to in more recent times.

How did this ancient region in Europe create a trendy adjective? Well, it all relates to a group of people who settled in Bohemia, that being the Romani people. Initially, to be described as "bohemian" was negative, as the lifestyles of the Romani people were seen as weird and unconventional to many people, and as they lived in Bohemia, their style of living became known as "bohemian." Eventually, over the years and thanks to a change in attitudes, many people wanted to start living an unconventional life like these people. Before we knew it, bohemian was the adjective everyone was pining to be described as; a certain rhapsody also may have helped in popularizing the word.

CARTHAGE

If there was ever an empire that came closest to dethroning Rome, it was the Carthaginian Empire. Much like the Roman Empire, their empire's name was simply the name of their capital city in adjective form, with that capital being Carthage. The city of Carthage lay in the north of modern-day Tunisia, though their empire spread across North Africa and even into southern Spain. All that lay between Carthage and Rome was the Mediterranean Sea and the islands of Italy, which of course Carthage tried to claim at various times. The disputes between Carthage and Rome came to a head in a series of wars called the Punic Wars, the second of which was perhaps the closest Rome came to being conquered. It was in the Second Punic War that Carthaginian General Hannibal Barca took elephants across Spain and over the Alps in an attempt to capture Rome. Rome had the last laugh though as the third and final Punic War resulted

31

in absolute defeat for Carthage and their lands being claimed by Rome.

Carthage has a simple meaning. It comes from the Phoenician *quart khadash*, which means "new town," as when Carthage was first set up, it was a new town. A simple name, that's for sure, but not a future-proof one; it won't be a new town forever! What you may have noticed also is the word *Punic*. This is the adjective used to describe things and people from Carthage. It might sound odd that these words are so different, but we still have instances of this on our planet today. Think how people and things from The Netherlands are described as Dutch. *Punic* is a word that came around just by being passed through languages. These people were also known as Phoenicians (as were other tribes from this part of the world) and over the years Phoenicians became *Punic*.

TAWANTINSUYU

I wouldn't be surprised if you had never heard of this one. I hadn't either before I started writing this book. What I am sure might sound way more familiar is the Inca Empire, and Tawantinsuyu is the name for their empire in their native tongue of Quechua. This name is sometimes seen spelt as two words instead of one, *Tawantin Suyu*, and it's from these two separate words that we can start making more sense of this name. The *tawantin* part in Quechua means "four," and the *suyu* part means things such as "realms/regions/province," so the name collectively can be translated into meaning the four realms. Suyu was a name for a type of region unto itself. The empire had this name because it was split into four main regions in the cardinal directions. It consisted of Chinchaysuyu in the north, Antisuyu in the east, Qullasuyu in the south, and Kuntisuyu in the west.

So, where did *Inca* come from? Well, *Inca* was a name used by the Incans themselves. While we would presume that all residents of the former Inca Empire would be considered Incans, that wasn't the case. Only the elite and ruling class of Inca society had the term applied to them. This is why the word *Inca* in Quechua means "ruler/lord." Not all Incas were Incas! Though once the Spanish and other European settlers arrived in what we now call South America, they would have primarily talked to the ruling class of the empire there, found out they called themselves Incas and would go on to mislabel the entire population as Incas.

CHEROKEE NATION

From South America to North America, the Cherokee Nation is an outlier in this chapter as it still exists. It just exists in a much smaller, reduced state than it once did. The original Cherokee Nation was around from 1794 till 1907 and was pretty much an entirely autonomous, tribal nation in North America that coexisted with the United States of America. The main residents of the Cherokee Nation were unsurprisingly the Cherokee indigenous people. Today, the land that made up this nation is now a part of the state of Oklahoma, with the smaller Cherokee Nation still being within this state.

To understand this one, we need to find out where the name Cherokee came from. There's a handful of ideas. One is that it comes from a different native language, the Creek tongue, meaning, in their language, "people of different speech." Another idea is that it comes from the Choctaw people and means "people who live in the mountains." It doesn't seem particularly fair that other tribes got to name these people; what if they wanted to name themselves?! Well luckily, they did! And to make things even better, the Cherokee name for Cherokees sounds nothing like Cherokee. It is instead *Aniyunwiya*. What's great about this name is that, unlike Cherokee, we know exactly what it means, and it means "principle people."

PANGEA

We are going further back than we have done so far, before we humans were even around and before the world even looked like it does now: this is the supercontinent of Pangea. All the land on our earth was, once upon a time, connected. You can kind of still see it too; South American's east coast looks like it could fit snugly into Africa's west coast. Pangea is the name we have given this huge hunk of land. It's thought to have existed 335 million to 175 million years ago. So yes, this place is rather old indeed!

Obviously, no one was around calling this land Pangea at the time; there were literally no humans around to call it anything. This name is a fairly recent concoction; the concept of Pangea itself was only created in 1912, just over one hundred years ago. Pangea is the brainchild of German geophysicist Alfred Wegener, though he didn't give the land a German name but instead opted to give it a name of Greek origin, as these things often get given Greek or Latin names to make them sound far fancier. *Pan* in Greek means "all/entire/whole," and the *gea* part relates to Gaia. In Greek mythology, Gaia is one of the primordial deities and is seen as the personification of earth. Gaia is often seen as an alternative name for the earth. This means that the name Pangea means "the entire earth" as the land of Pangea did, in fact, consist of the entire earth.

Bodies of Water

In the last volume, we spent an awful lot of time looking into the names of things that were on land: countries, cities, landmarks. While there is an awful lot of land on our earth, it only accounts for around 30 percent of the entire surface. The other 70 percent belongs to perhaps the most important thing for us humans: water. Water takes many forms on our planet, from mighty oceans to gentle streams. This time around, let's celebrate the planet's life-giving liquid and look into how just a few of the earth's various bodies of water got their names.

PACIFIC OCEAN

The Pacific Ocean is the largest body of water on our planet. At over sixty million square miles in size, it's unfathomably huge. It stretches across from Australia, New Zealand, and Eastern Asia, all the way across to the Americas. One source pointed out that if you wanted to sail across this entire ocean, it would take about five to ten weeks, and that's with favourable winds! This is a body of water not to be taken lightly. Yet, despite its sheer magnitude, its name is rather pleasant, serene, and quite literally peaceful.

37

Pacific comes from Spanish and Portuguese roots meaning "peaceful," and it's a word we see in other parts of language like the verb pacify, meaning "to bring something to peace." Or pacifier, the name Americans use for the thing you put in babies' mouths to make them more peaceful. How did these vast waters end up with a name meaning peaceful? Well, it dates back to the explorations of Portuguese navigator Ferdinand

Magellan (who was employed by Spain) in the sixteenth century. He was charting waters that had not been fully explored yet. His adventures had been turbulent and perilous, with raging seas that threatened to capsize his entire fleet. Eventually, however, he and his crew found themselves in much calmer and more peaceful waters. Grateful for these calmer waters, he dubbed them *Mar Pacífico*, which means "peaceful sea," and while we now know it's an ocean, not a sea, the peaceful part of the name stuck around.

Clearly, he wasn't boastful enough to name the ocean after himself; however, some water has been named after him, that being the Strait of Magellan in southern Chile; it was this strait Magellan had to navigate to reach the Pacific's peaceful waters.

YANGTZE RIVER

This river has a somewhat unique claim to fame; it's the longest river to run entirely within one country. It's almost four thousand miles long too, so it has to be a pretty big country to fit this massive river entirely within its borders and a pretty big country it is, indeed. The Yangtze River calls the nation of China its home. As well as being the largest river in one country, it is also the largest in Asia, and third in the world! As this river is so long, and China is so ancient, it means that before it was realised that this was one huge river, various parts of the Yangtze had been given unique names. This includes *Chang Jiang*, meaning "long river" for one section of it. *Jinsha Jiang* means "gold sands river" for another part. *Tongtian* means "river passing through heaven." And even *Tuotuo*, which means "tearful river."

Though none of these names explain the name used for the entire river, Yangtze. This name is thought to most likely be a European concoction, believed to come from an old Ferry Crossing called *Yángzǐ* in the Yangzhou province. So the river was named after this crossing, and this crossing was named after the region. Europeans must have arrived at this part and named the river after the port. While that might not be the most exciting thing, there's something unique about this. A huge amount of places are named after rivers that run through them, so to have a river named after the region it's in is unique, indeed!

CARIBBEAN SEA

Is there anywhere else on our planet that conjures up an image quite like the Caribbean? Blazing sunshine, exotic wildlife, sunny beaches, pirates hunting for treasure. Now obviously, the Caribbean Sea is way more than just these generic stereotypes and tropes. It's a part of the world with a deep, dark history and is seen as the gateway to the New World. It was an island in what we now call The Bahamas that Columbus first landed on, paving the way for European interaction with the Americas.

This island was named *Guanahani* by the natives there; Columbus, however, went on to rename it San Salvador. Replacing the native names of places in the Caribbean with names of his choice is something Columbus did rather liberally. Luckily, the sea in which his "discoveries" took place doesn't have a name of his creation, though he did try. The land within the sea he called Antillas, with the sea taking the title Sea of Antilles. Columbus initially thought he was in India, though upon realising he wasn't, called the area the West Indies as it lay west to the East Indies from a European perspective.

Caribbean is luckily a word that derives from origins native to the Caribbean. That being with the Carib people, who are native to some of the smaller islands in the sea. Caribbean is an adjective meaning "relating to the Caribs," so when we say "Caribbean Sea," we are saying "the sea of the Carib." Unfortunately, though, despite being a name of natives, Caribs is the Spanish corruption of their name. In their native tongue, they are known as *Kalinago*, which means "brave/strong ones."

LAKE SUPERIOR

As the largest freshwater lake by some measures on the entire planet, I can assure you that Lake Superior suits having that name. While we link the word superior with meaning "better/higher in quality," it has another meaning that somewhat relates to these meanings. The word superior comes from the French *supérieur*, meaning "upper," and Lake Superior was initially called *Lac Supérieur* as it was named by the French; this lake does share a border with Canada. The French didn't call it superior just because of its vast size but also because it was the uppermost lake of all the Great Lakes. It's worth remembering that the French were not the first to name this lake; before them, the native Ojibwe people called this lake Gichi-Gami, which means "great sea," so even these guys were enamoured by its huge size.

LAKE DISAPPOINTMENT

Unfortunately, not every lake can be superior. Some lakes are rather disappointing. This lake in the middle of the sparse Pilbara region of Australia was seen as so disappointing it was named after the fact! This name was given to the lake by explorer Frank Hann in 1897. Imagine exploring this dry, arid part of the world in the nineteenth century with limited water and the sun blazing down on you. It would be pretty gruelling, that's for sure. While treading through this land, Frank started to notice small creeks; he was sure these creeks would lead to a freshwater lake where he could quench his thirst and cool off. Much to his disappointment, however, these creeks merely led to a dry saltwater lake instead, far from the oasis he had in mind. Angered by his discovery, he branded the lake with the silly name of Lake Disappointment. In 2020, much like with many of Australia's sights, the lake's native name was given back to it. The lake is now formally called Kumpupintil Lake. This name describes how the lake was created, which involves ancient warriors in an epic battle with giants; it's a far less disappointing name, that's for sure!

47

PRETTYBOY RESERVOIR

Reservoir itself comes from the French *réservoir*, meaning "storehouse," and eventually, the word took on a broader meaning of anything that can store anything, and a water-based reservoir is a place to collect/store water. The verb of reserve comes from the same French roots too, as it means to hold on to something. It's an interesting word with an interesting etymology, though I am pretty sure the reservoir part of the name isn't the part that struck you as interesting first.

This reservoir can be found in the state of Maryland over in the USA as part of the Gunpowder River. It wasn't named after a human boy who was pretty though. Instead, it was named after something literally with the name Prettyboy—this literal Prettyboy being a horse. Well, I say literal, but this name comes from a local legend. The story goes that a farmer who lived nearby had a colt called Prettyboy. Prettyboy was beloved by the local community. However, one stormy night, the farm was hit by a flash flood, which swept the horse away into the Gunpowder River, never to be seen again. The farmer and the community were heartbroken by the loss of their beloved Prettyboy, so when the reservoir was constructed, it was named in honour of the lost horse. We, of course, don't know how much truth there is in this story; however, it's a wonderful story nevertheless, and it's a darn good reason to name a reservoir, regardless of its validity.

LAKE VÄTTERN

While not the largest lake in Sweden, Lake Vättern is well-known for another reason. The water of this lake is incredibly clear and clean. You can regularly see up to fifteen meters below the water's surface with your own eyes, and its water is so clean you can drink it straight away without worrying about pests or hygiene. The lake is enjoyed for its sights, boat trips, and it's a rather good fishing spot too.

There's a couple of ideas as to where this name may come from, one boring and one more exciting. The more boring one is the idea that it comes from the Swedish term *vatten*, which means "water." As I said, it's not the most thrilling idea. You don't have to be the most creative person to name a huge body of water after water. The more exciting idea is that it comes from the ancient term of *vätter*, meaning "lake spirit." I much prefer this idea, and it seems an especially fitting name for a lake so crystal clear. I can just imagine ancient Norsemen being amazed at the clear, beautiful waters of this lake and presuming that the only way it could be so well kept was thanks to spirited, enchanting waters. It's an idea that makes you feel spirited away, if you pardon the pun.

LOCH NESS

In the wild north of Scotland, you will find the mysterious waters of Loch Ness. A "loch" (which is just a Celtic term for a lake) known across the world thanks to its cryptic inhabitant, the Loch Ness Monster. People all across the globe, from scientists to monster enthusiasts, have visited Loch Ness to try and catch a glimpse of Nessie or even prove once and for all that the beast is real. Is Nessie real, though? Well, that's not for me to say. While it may not be the biggest loch or body of water in the UK—or even just Scotland, for that matter—it does have incredible depths, reaching 230 meters at its deepest point. I imagine it's these deep waters that have convinced so many people that something or someone must be lurking down there.

Anyway, I'll take off my tinfoil hat for now. I'm just here to explain that name. Loch Ness is simply named after the river that flows out of it called the River Ness. As for where the river got its name, well, it's thought to come from an old Celtic word meaning "roaring one." I guess this roaring relates to the roaring sound of the water. Though maybe it doesn't relate to the sound of the water but instead relates to the roar of the ancient creature that hides in the waters. We can't be sure.

There is a second idea as to where this name comes from, which relates to roaring too, though not the roaring of waters or the roaring of a mythical creature, but the roaring of the locals who would have to flee in storms where the waters of the loch started to rise. The story goes that in these storms, people would shout, *"Tha loch 'nis ann, tha loch 'nis ann!"* which translates in English as, "There is a lake there now, there is a lake there now!" and it was the *"loch 'nis"* part of this shouting that became the name, "Loch Ness."

BAY OF PIGS

The Bay of Pigs might be more known for historical reasons as the site of a failed invasion, but first and foremost, it is a body of water in the island nation of Cuba. Both parts of its name, however, are something of a lie. First, it's more of an inlet than an actual bay, and second, you won't find any pigs in the Bay of Pigs, at least not the snout-nosed and curly-tailed kind of pigs that I am sure we are all thinking of.

The Spanish name for this bay is *Bahía de los Cochinos*, and I am sure you can see that the first part of this name means "bay of." It's the last word of this Spanish name that is of most interest to us, *cochinos*. This word can mean pig in Spanish; however, it is also the name for a type of fish found in the waters around Cuba. In English, it is known as the "triggerfish." Why Spanish uses the same name for these and the pink mammals, however, we aren't too sure. I imagine it's to do with the fact that the triggerfish's little mouth looks somewhat like a pig's snout. Either way, it's thought that the pigs in the name the Bay of Pigs relates to these fish as opposed to the tasty animals. I suppose a more fitting translation of the bay's name in English would be The Bay of Triggerfish, but that's nowhere near as fun.

45

RIVER NILE

The longest river on our planet stretches over four thousand miles in length and runs through ten countries. The country it's most associated with is, of course, Egypt, where its fertile banks allowed ancient Egyptians to not only grow crops for eating but papyrus too for turning into baskets, rope, and, most importantly, paper, which allowed Egypt to become the incredible civilization it was. The Nile has played important roles in religions too, from the Egyptian god Hapi, who was responsible for flooding the river each year to baby Moses being set adrift down the Nile for his own protection. It is quite possibly the most well-known river on our planet.

It is such a definitive river on our planet that many think that its name means simply that, "river." Coming from the Semitic *nahal*, meaning "river," this idea is the correct etymology. That means when I say "the River Nile," what I am saying is "the River River." This is something known as a tautological place name, which is when a place name is the same word twice but in different languages. It makes sense as to why this river would just be called river though. To the ancient Egyptians and other ancient people, this river would have been so vast and important to them. It was most likely the only river they would have known of or seen, so it wouldn't have needed a more definitive name, as there wouldn't have been any other rivers to compare it to or get it confused with. If you just said the river, people would know you are talking about the Nile!

It's thought that the ancient Egyptians probably wouldn't have called it the Nile, however. Instead, they would have used their word for river, which is thought to have been *iteru*. Eventually, the ancient tongue was replaced with a language called Coptic, and the Coptic word for river is *piaro*, so this would have been the river's name too. The

Egyptians' most famous form of language were their hieroglyphs, and the hieroglyphic name for the river is thought to have been a quill/feather, followed by an oval with a semi-circle above it, followed by a bird, followed by three zigzag lines on top of each other. Simply describing these glyphs doesn't quite do them justice, I am well aware. Luckily, through the power of technology, I can show you these symbols! Though this won't benefit the audiobook listeners.

Plants

Take a look at any picture of our planet, and there will be two dominant colours, blue and green. The blue obviously comes from the fantastic bodies of water we just spent a whole chapter gushing over. The green, however, comes from the wonderful plants on our planet. Plants can take on all sorts of forms, so many in fact that I have split them into two chapters, as you will see once we are done here. Right now, I want to focus on the smaller side of the green kingdom, like the flowers we give to those we love or the plants we litter our houses with. Here, I have aimed to share with you the origins of some of the most known plants on our planet, as well as bring to light some odd plant names you may have never heard before.

DAISY

The humble daisy. It often gets overlooked in the world of flowers. While it may not be as pretty or extravagant as other flowers, its humble, simple appearance has made it somewhat the archetypal flower in the minds and eyes of many people. Speaking of eyes, the name daisy actually relates to eyes.

49

Daisy is a name of Old English roots, a combination of the Old English words *dæges* and *eage*, which in modern English means "day's eye." The modern name Daisy sounds awfully like day's eye now that I look at it. But why is a daisy the day's eye? Well, first off, just look at them. With their petals forming a circle of white with a ball of colour in the middle, they do look a lot like eyes—cartoon eyes, anyway. I don't think anyone's actual eyes are just white and yellow with no pupils. But why do these eyes belong to just the day? Well, during the day, these flowers burst open, yet at nighttime, they close up again. They only look like eyes during the day. They are the day's eye.

The words of the fancy Latin name of *Bellis perennis* mean "pretty" and "everlasting," respectively. This is simply because not only are these flowers pretty, they're pretty hardy too and are rather long-lasting.

VENUS FLYTRAP

We all know that plants are living beings just like you and me, despite the fact they may lack certain things we consider important, like eyes or a brain. Though undeniably, one plant that looks strikingly alive is the Venus flytrap. This is thanks to their gaping mouth-like leaves that attract small insects for these flowers to devour! It's no wonder so many works of fiction have been inspired by these plants, from *Little Shop of Horrors* to Super Mario's Piranha Plants—there are plants out there that can eat flesh! Luckily, none have a taste for humans, yet.

The flytrap part of this name should be pretty self-explanatory, though they eat way more than just flies. Any insect that finds its way into the plant's maw is fair game. The Venus part of the name will undoubtedly ring a bell with the mythology fans among us. Venus is the name of the Roman goddess of love and beauty; her Greek equivalent is Aphrodite. This monstrous plant is named after such a beautiful being because the plants themselves are rather pretty too. These plants use their good looks to attract insects into visiting their leaves, and before you know it, dinner is served!

BAMBOO

If you have peeked ahead to the next chapter of this book, then you may be wondering why I am covering bamboo here. Well, while it is rather woody and is used in the same way as wood in many cases, bamboo is a kind of grass. While bamboo grows all over our planet, it is most heavily associated with Asia, especially nations like China and Japan. Despite being such a universally recognised type of plant, we aren't too sure where its name came from. Luckily, we have some ideas. It's thought to be a European corruption of a word from an Asian language. Though what European language and what Asian language, we don't seem to agree upon. The general consensus is that originally it's a word from the Asian Malay language that was corrupted by European Spanish or Portuguese. In Malay, the word was initially *mambu* before it was corrupted into bamboo by Europeans. Though I also read that in Malay, the word was *bambu* and has an onomatopoeic origin. Apparently, when bamboo is set on fire, it makes a bamboo sound due to being hollow on the inside. You may have to check this one out for yourselves, as I have no spare bamboo to hand to set alight to right now, I'm afraid.

51

ALOE VERA

Walk into any pharmacy or cosmetics shop and I have no doubt you will find at least one ointment with this plant's name slapped on the front, and that's for a good reason. Aloe vera is a plant with remarkable medicinal properties. It keeps your skin clean and hydrated, helps relieve heartburn, and works as a natural laxative. While the plant and the satisfying gel found within its leaves have a huge amount of uses, unfortunately, it's not a simple wonder cure that can heal any issue the human body may be facing. People of the past, however, thought this was the case.

The ancient Egyptians dubbed aloe vera the plant of immortality, and the ancient Greeks thought it was the universal panacea, a name for something that could cure all diseases. The words that make up this name reflect this idea that it could cure anything and everything. Aloe vera is a part of a larger family of plants called aloes, so the first part of this name reflects its family. One idea as to where the word aloe comes from is with Arabic, and their word of *alloeh*, which means "shining bitter substance" in reference to the plant's gel. The vera part comes from Latin and means "true," as aloe vera is the truest form of pants in the aloe family. I also imagine that this trueness relates to its healing properties; it's the one true plant that can heal all!

The name aloe vera relates to another name, the first name of Veronica. One idea behind the name Veronica is that it comes from the Latin phrase *vera icon*, which means "true image." This true image is an image of Jesus that appeared on a woman's veil. This etymology means that the vera in aloe vera and the vera that created Veronica are one and the same. Well, if that etymology is true that is, pardon the pun.

MONSTERA DELICIOSA

You will often find this plant not so much out in the wild or in a lovely garden, but in a pot in someone's living room, as *monstera deliciosa* is a common kind of house plant. You probably won't see it with that name, however, in the house plant store (I think that's a thing), as that is its fancy Latin name. This name is pretty easy to understand. The first word in this name obviously means "monster," and that's because of the monstrous sizes that these plants can reach. They are able to grow as high as nine meters! The latter word means "delicious," and that's because this plant produces fruit that, when eaten unripe, is foul and can even irritate your throat, but when eaten at the perfect time is, in fact, rather delicious!

Though, as I mentioned, you won't see this plant for sale under that name. Instead, you may see it called the Swiss cheese plant. While Swiss cheese is delicious, its fruit doesn't taste like it, unfortunately. Vegans would have a field day if that was the case. This plant is named after Swiss cheese not because of its taste but because of its look. The leaves are full of holes and look somewhat like the cheese idolised by cartoon mice, hence why it's named after the dairy product.

MOTHER-IN-LAWS TONGUE

Mothers-in-law seem to so often get a bad rap in society, most noticeably the butt of many jokes. There's even a whole Wikipedia article about mother-in-law jokes, which explains how mothers-in-law are often depicted as overbearing, harsh, and ugly! In reality, the personalities of mothers-in-law vary from person to person. I am sure there are just as many loving in-laws as there are unpleasant in-laws. Nevertheless, this stereotype has entrenched itself enough in our society that even a plant has been named after the trope—the mother-in-law's tongue.

This is another popular houseplant; if you look at this plant, you will notice the shape and sharpness of its leaves. These leaves reminded people of the metaphorically sharp tongues of mothers-in-law, so the plant was named after them. It's also worth mentioning that mother-in-law's tongue is just one name the plant goes by. It's also known as the snake plant and Saint George's Sword, both of which relate to the sharpness of its leaves.

COSMOS

This is a word that will fill a lot of people with a sense of wonder. Cosmos can easily conjure up an image of the night sky, shooting stars, distant planets, and a whole nebula of adventures. It can also conjure up a different image too, that being of small flowers of varying shades of pink to orange. As well as being a term for our night sky, cosmos is also the name for a type of flower. I have to wonder, is there any connection between the two?

Well, surprisingly, yes! Before being the name for the universe or a type of flower, it was originally the Greek word *kosmos*, which meant "balance, order, harmony." Greek philosopher Pythagoras (yes, the one you hated in maths class) is believed to have first applied the word to the universe and earth. He believed the universe was in a perfect balance, hence why he applied the word to it. At some point, the word started being spelt with a C instead of a K. It was the C spelling that Spanish explorers used when they came across these flowers in their native Mexico. When they arrived back in Spain, priests took a keen fascination in them. They were impressed at how evenly placed the flower petals were. You could even say that the flower's petals were in perfect harmony or balance with one another. It was because of this harmony between their petals as to how and why they got this word of cosmos applied to them too.

This Greek word for balance and harmony hasn't only appeared in the name of these things. It also created the word cosmetic. It's a word we must link with beauty and making something look more beautiful. Cosmetic products are used to make people feel more attractive; the same goes for cosmetic surgery. While that original Greek word means "balance and harmony," it's not a stretch to see how this got applied to meaning beautiful too. We often see things that are balanced and perfect as being beautiful, like our universe or even these flowers.

SNEEZEWORT

The name of this plant sounds more like it's from the pages of a fairytale than the pages of any botany book. It sounds like something a witch would pepper into a bubbling cauldron. I can assure you, however, that sneezewort is indeed a real type of plant. Though sneezewort is more a colloquial name for it, its actual fancy Latin name is *achillea ptarmica*, with the first part of this name being an ode to the Greek hero Achilles. The latter part means "causing sneezing," so even in its proper name, it relates to sneezes! This name is seemingly justified, however, as I have read that this plant's flower gives off a unique pungent smell that can lead to sneezing in some people.

Why a wort? This is a word element we see in many plant names. It has nothing to do with the lumps of skin; they are spelt with an "a." Wort is simply an Old English term for plants, coming from *wyrt*. What's interesting is that I read that plants deemed to be beneficial were given the name of wort, whereas plants seen as having no use and generally as being a pain were called weeds. Wort as a word for good plants may have fallen out of fashion, but weed is here to stay. Also, does this mean sneezewort was seen as a good thing? Sneezing has its benefits, I suppose; sneezeweed does have a nice ring to it though.

MONEY PLANT

There's an old saying, "Money doesn't grow on trees," and while that is unfortunately the case, what about money growing on a different kind of plant? While there's seemingly no money flower or money bush, we do have a money plant! Don't get too excited, however, as I am afraid that despite the name, money plants don't produce any money. This houseplant is named after money for the simple reason that its leaves look somewhat like money, which I can kind of see. Its leaves by no means are golden or have the face of someone important on them, but they are round and thick and somewhat reminiscent of coins.

It is also known as the "jade plant," and this name ties into the name "money plant" too. Its leaves are said to be not only similar in shape to coins but also similar in shape to jade coins of ancient China. Thanks to this, another prophecy has begun about this plant—as long as this plant is growing well, then its owner shall financially prosper. With a story like that, it's easy to see how this has become one of the world's most popular house plants.

57

ORCHIDS

Orchids are some of the most desirable and beloved flowers on our planet; their name, however, isn't as desirable. What would you name a flower this pretty after? Sunsets? Rainbows? Puppies? Well, they aren't named after anything like that. Instead, the Greeks created their names from their word órkhis, which means "testicle," as in the thing between the legs of men. Yep, orchids are named after balls.

How did this happen? Well, it has nothing to do with the flowers themselves but more to do with what's happening underground. Orchids grow from a tuber, a large growth in its roots that can store water and nutrients for the flower to live off during harsher conditions. Potatoes are a type of tuber. Orchid tubers come in pairs and are small and round and reminiscent of you-know-what, hence how this pretty flower ended up with a naughty name. If you thought it couldn't get any more raunchy, well, guess what their name in Middle English was? Bollockwort.

Trees

The flora of our planet is way more than pretty plants and dainty flowers. Perhaps the most important plants on our planet are the trees. Trees are seen as our planet's lungs and make so much of the oxygen we need to survive. They are pretty darn important and deserve a chapter of their own in this book! What's great about trees is that there isn't just one type of them, from huge trees that tower over all things to tiny things that line gardens. I hope to cover a variety of trees here, from the well-known and loved to some of the more bizarre. Let's get to the root of these tree etymologies! I promise that's the only time I'll use that pun in this chapter.

SEQUOIA

Why not kick things off with the largest type of tree on our planet? Sequoia is a shortening of their full name, which is Giant Sequoia. I am pretty sure you don't need me to explain the giant part of this name though. These trees are not only unfathomably tall but can be unfathomably old too, reaching thousands of years in age. Despite being so big, they only naturally occur in a specific area. They can only be found in the wild on the western slopes of the Sierra Nevada mountains in California—as I said, specific!

These American trees have a name with an American origin. It's believed the tree was named after a Cherokee Native American called Sequoyah. Why him in particular? Well, he played an important role for the Cherokees in that he singlehandedly created a writing system for the Cherokee language so that the tongue could be read and written, which is incredibly impressive, as I am sure you will all agree. Though, what has creating a writing system got to do with trees? Well, not an awful lot, in all honesty. Though the botanist who named the tree in honour of the native, the German Steven Endlicher, was also a student of linguistics. A botanist *and* a linguist? I am sure he lived quite a rock 'n' roll lifestyle. As Endlicher studied this great American tree and came to the conclusion that it was a unique species, he wanted to name it after a great figure in American history. Considering he was a student of linguistics, it makes sense that the figure of American history he would name it after would relate to the world of languages.

This name of Sequoia fits the tree in another way too. It could be seen as relating to the Latin *sequi*, meaning "to follow," which fits the tree as its seeds fit the mathematical flow of other trees in its family. I'm not too sure; the invention of the Cherokee alphabet story is much more fun I am sure you will all agree. This tree has had other names too; it is popularly also known as the giant Redwood, which is a name early Spanish settlers in the states called it too, though in their native Spanish, of course, *Palo colorado*.

61

PAUBRASILIA

From a distinctly North American tree to a distinctly South American tree, Portuguese explorers found this tree during their explorations of South America. They instantly recognised this tree as a relative of the Sappanwood tree found in Asia. The Sappanwood had an important use to the people of Europe; it was through these trees that red dye was produced, meaning people could quite literally paint the town red, among other things. As this new tree related to that tree, it meant this one could be used to make red dye too, and suddenly a new source for the colour red was found. The Portuguese wasted no time in naming their new tree, dubbing in the paubrasilia, which comes from their words for wood and red/amber.

This tree was so vital to the Portuguese that eventually their land in South America became named after them, initially calling their claimed territory on the continent *Terra do Brasil*, meaning Land of Paubrasilia. This name was, of course, eventually shortened to just Brazil, hence how the nation got its name. And this tree is now also known as the brazilwood tree, but I think if I started this section by calling it that, where this story was going would have been even more obvious.

SYCAMORE

This name has been applied to a variety of trees. The most popular kind of tree with this name is the *Acer pseudoplatanus*, which is known as just a Sycamore in British English but is called a Sycamore Maple in American English. The first kind of tree to have this name however was the *Ficus sycomorus*, which is native to Africa and the Middle East. This type of tree produced figs and was named by the Greeks, as in ancient Greece figs were called *sykon*. While that explains the first part of the name, what about the "more" part?

Well luckily, I can tell you a lot more about it! Pun intended. The "more" in this name comes from the *morus* genus of trees, also known as mulberries. Sycamore trees were named after mulberry trees because the leaves of these initial fig-producing sycamore trees were similar in shape to the leaves of mulberry trees. So sycamore means "mulberry-leaved fig tree," meaning it's a tree named after its fruit and another kind of tree. What makes things even more confusing is that this name has since been applied to other trees that have different-shaped leaves and don't even produce figs. It's all silly and confusing, that's for sure; no more sycamore talk.

MONKEY PUZZLE TREE

This evergreen tree has a more sensible name, that being the Chilean Pine, named because it's a type of pine tree native to the country of Chile. Here in the UK, however, it goes by the name of the monkey puzzle tree, and there's one word I can use to describe that name: puzzling. I can understand why a tree would be named after monkeys, as more often than not monkeys are seen swinging through trees. In fact, another name for this tree is the monkey trail tree, which makes sense as the branches of this tree are reminiscent of the tails of monkeys like gibbons and capuchins. While these trees are of Chilean origin, the name of "monkey puzzle" is a British invention.

There's a neat little story behind this name. The tree supposedly came to the shores of Britain in 1850. The specimen was bought by Sir William Molesworth, a politician who also had an interest in botany. He purchased the tree in his later years and had it planted in the gardens of his house in Cornwall. Eager to show off his latest purchase, he brought a group of his friends over to gawk at this foreign tree. Monkey puzzle trees have sharp, pointed leaves on sporadic branches. They aren't the most ordinary kind of trees, that's for sure. Its bizarre leaves and branches led one of Molesworth's guests, Charles Austin, to say, "That tree would puzzle a monkey" in relation to how the monkey would try to figure out how to climb the thing. Clearly, Molesworth was so tickled by his friend's response to the tree that he decided to name it in honour of this odd statement. At first, the trees were called "monkey puzzlers" before being shortened to just "monkey puzzle."

JOSHUA TREE

This is one for the U2 fans reading this book, though the tree's etymology has nothing to do with the band I'm afraid. In fact, these trees might not even be trees at all; nevertheless, we are going to talk about them here. These trees are thought to have a name of religious origins. They are only found in the southwest of the United States, and the legend goes that in the mid-nineteenth century, Mormon settlers were exploring the land. It is said that the tree's branches looked like arms reaching out, and these branches reminded these Mormons of Joshua from the Bible. In Joshua 8:18, he holds his arms out wide to help guide Israelites during a conquest. The tree reminded them of Joshua's actions, so, in turn, named it after him. I must stress that this is just a theory, perhaps even just a folk tale. Still, it's a fun story.

These trees have the more official name of yucca trees; this is because they belong to the genus of yucca. Though this name is seemingly just as confusing; the genus of yucca plants was mistaken with the cassava which are also known as yucca, so this name was mistakenly given to these plants too. So, we have a plant called yucca, which isn't a yucca. And plants that are yuccas that don't use the name are, like I said, confusing.

WEEPING WILLOW

Don't worry, guys; the tree isn't crying. It's just the name. A crying tree would be an awful sight, that's for sure. Though with the long drooping branches of this tree, it's easy to see why people would think they are crying. Weeping willows do give off a sombre vibe, and that name doesn't help. They look even more tearful when it rains too; as it rains, the water runs down their branches like tears. It's thanks to this phenomenon as to why these willows are known for weeping.

65

That's the easy part of the name; where does the word willow come from? It's a word we link so much with trees and nature. This is a pretty ancient word of obscure Germanic roots. It's forebear words include the likes of *wilgia*, *wilghe*, and *wilg* in Old Saxon, Old Dutch, and Dutch, respectively. It's ultimately thought to maybe come from an ancient word meaning "to turn/revolve," which could maybe relate to their winding trunks and branches, though that's just my guess. The fancy Latin word for willow is *salix*, and this comes from Latin words meaning "near water," as a lot of the time, you will find these trees exactly where you think this name implies they'll be.

ELM

Elm might seem like an odd little word, but the beauty of a word is that an interesting etymology can be hiding behind even just three little letters, and that's the case with the word elm. Elm is thought to come from old roots meaning "reddish-brown," which is understandably meant to relate to the tree's colour. The tree definitely lands more on the brown side of reddish-brown, but I can see some red in there, I suppose. What's cool about this name is that it was this old word meaning reddish-brown that gave something else its name too, elk. Think about it; elk is awfully similar to the word elm, and like the tree, these mammals are a reddish-brown colour too. There's just something I find so cool about a woodland creature, and the woodland itself has a name from the same root. If you ever see an elk next to an elm, then now you know these two things have more in common than you may have thought at first!

BAOBAB

These trees are almost alien-looking; however, they are native to Africa, most noticeably on the island of Madagascar. Their huge thick trunks with a scattering of branches up top are certainly a sight to behold. Sometimes, they are even known as upside-down trees, as their branches look somewhat like roots and their actual branches are under the earth. This upside-down image has even led to myths about the tree being plucked up by the devil and shoved back into the ground the wrong way. One story even says that this tree was one of God's first creations, and it wouldn't stop following him around, so it was God who picked it up and buried it head-first. Though that nickname has nothing to do with their actual name.

Baobab is a name of Arabic origin. Initially, in Arabic, they were called *abū ḥibāb*, meaning "father of many seeds," and over the years this name became "baobab." It's understandable as to why it would have this name—despite the myths of it being buried the wrong way around and being a tad goofy, this is a truly magnificent-looking tree. I saw it called the tree of life in one source, and it does just give off an image of being one of the more mighty trees in the land. To imagine it as the father tree to everything else isn't too much of a stretch, especially for ancient peoples. Its official name of *adansonia* doesn't have quite as mystical origins. This name comes from French naturalist Michel Adanson, who studied the trees extensively.

67

DRAGON BLOOD TREE

Just when you thought these tree names couldn't get any more weird, we have the dragon blood tree. The way these trees' branches all grow in an upright dome shape make them look more like giant alien mushrooms than trees. This tree is so unique that it's only found in one part of the world, the Socotra Islands off the coast of Yemen.

What can't be found on these far-off islands, however, are actual dragons.

How did this tree in the Arabian sea end up being named after the blood of a mythological beast? Well, it's all to do with the tree's sap. While tree sap is often a yellow to brown colour, that isn't quite the case with these guys. Their sap is a deep blood red. You can see pictures of people carving into these trees and red fluid gushing out of them as if they are bleeding! Why dragon's blood, though? Well, that's up for interpretation. I think, due to the uniqueness of these trees and their exotic location, dragons are the only animal blood that's fair to compare their sap to. It would be underwhelming if you travelled across the blazing Arabian Peninsula and found this tree in its exclusive natural habitat, only to find out it's called the mouse blood tree.

BONSAI

I guess bonsai might be considered more an art form than a type of tree, but it's an art form that revolves around trees. Bonsai isn't the name for one particular species of tree; instead, it's the name of all purposefully grown and cultivated miniature trees. They come in all shapes and—err, I guess I can't say sizes there, can I? As they strictly come in just one size, small. It's a craft form that arrived out of Japan, and some of them are truly breathtaking.

Bonsai is a Japanese word for potted plants. As it arrived from the Japanese *bon,* meaning "pot," and the Japanese *sai*, meaning "to plant." This is because traditionally, you don't grow bonsai trees in the ground but rather in small pots, basins, and trays. It makes them all the more marvelous. Not only are they tiny trees, but they're tiny trees in tiny pots!

69

Buildings

That's enough gushing over things that can be found in the great outdoors; now, I want to celebrate the great indoors! The concept of being indoors is such a wonderful man-made construct. Having buildings is one of the defining things that separate us from the rest of the animal kingdom. All buildings are not made equal; however, buildings are constructed for a variety of reasons. Some we play in, some we work in, some we worship in, and some we buy things in, just to name a few uses we have found for buildings over the years. This chapter isn't so much for the specific names of specific buildings but rather the catchall names we use for different kinds of buildings.

SCHOOL

School is such an important time in many of our lives. It's where we meet our friends, learn about the world, and get shaped into the people we are going to become. It's undeniable that school isn't always the best time in everyone's life though. School can stress out so many kids and teachers alike, from the masses of homework to bullying. Everyone at some point probably found school to be a stressful, unlikeable place. What's so interesting about the word is its origins come from the exact opposite.

The name school ultimately derives from the Greek *skhole*, which means things like "spare time, leisure, ease, and rest." These are things I, for one, definitely do not link with school! The reason the word comes from this root is that many of the stressful, boring, worrisome things we do in school were things that the ancient Greeks did

71

for pleasure and in their spare time. Imagine having a day off and deciding what you wanted to do with it was some Pythagoras. Well, that's exactly what Greeks like Pythagoras did, hence why the theorem he created was named after him. As time went on, it was decided that these activities the Greeks did in their leisure were to be mandatory for all youth to partake in. This Greek word of *skhole* ended up being applied to the buildings, and the English word of "school" soon followed, along with the blazers, compasses, and the decades-old gum under the desk.

CINEMA

The theatre, the movies, the pictures, whatever you want to call it, the most definitive name for these buildings has to be cinema. Despite how much easier it has become over the years to watch films at home, people can't resist watching a film for the first time in the cinema. From the popcorn to the trailers, maybe it's one of mankind's best communal experiences. Well, as long as no one decides to talk on their phone for the entire film. What's interesting about this type of building is it's named after a single piece of equipment instrumental for their existence, the cinematograph. These were the original cameras designed by the French Lumière brothers that allowed our real world to not only be captured in motion but to be played back for all to see on the huge screen. Of course, modern filmmakers don't use these archaic cameras all too often these days. But the buildings that play their blockbusters are still named in honour of these devices.

While that's all well and good, it opens up another question for us, how did these cameras get their names? Well, as mentioned, their creators were French, so initially, this was the French word of *cinématographe*; however, this word comes from Greek elements. The first half of this name comes from *kinema*, which means "movement," and the latter half comes from the popular -graphy suffix, which means "to write," so the name means "to write down motion," which is a name with beauty behind it; the idea of being able to write down and record motion must have seemed mad to people of the past, but we were able to do it! Maybe I'm just too much of a film snob.

HOSPITAL

These buildings are perhaps the most important in our society; it's where many of our lives begin and where many of our lives may end. Few of us go our entire lives without ever having to visit a hospital. The word hospital ultimately derives from the Latin word of *hospes*. There's something rather unique about this word, and that's the variety of meanings it has. It's thought to have been the Latin word *hospes*, first meaning "host," as well as their word for things like "strangers, guests, or visitors." All these meanings for the word got mixed together and came to mean to host a guest or stranger. I am sure you can see how it ended up being applied to places where sick people recover, as most people in hospitals are strangers to those working there, yet they are hosted with the utmost respect. You could say that hospitals are hospitable!

73

That adjective of hospitable brings me to the next reason as to why that Latin word of *hospes* is so incredible, and that's because of how many other words we have derived from it. Not only do we have hospitable, but we have its noun form of hospitality. Hospitality is the collective name for a whole industry, which includes the likes of restaurants, bars, and theme parks because all these jobs involve hosting and caring for guests/strangers. So when someone says they work in hospitality, they are more likely to be taking food orders than taking x-rays.

The Latin *hospes* also gave us the name for another kind of building entirely, hotels. These are also named after the Latin word for "hosts/strangers," as hospitals and hotels also take care of guests. Though I imagine that the guests at hotels are a little happier to be there than the guests at hospitals—maybe hospitals should consider leaving chocolates on the pillows too.

DELICATESSEN

If you happen to be scratching your head in regard to what one of these is, you may be more aware of these buildings under their shortened name of deli. Delicatessens are wonderful stores that sell so many delicious treats, from cheeses to cured meats. Most delis will also bundle their products into sandwiches too. They are perhaps most closely associated with New York City. However, I am sure you can tell with that name that this name isn't of English origins. Delicatessens seem to be of German origin, and while this is their name in German, they got their name from the French *délicatesse,* which

came from the Italian *delicatezza,* which came from the
Latin word *delicatus.*

So to understand the name of these establishments, we
have to understand this Latin word, and in English, it
means things like "alluring" and "dainty." Dainty isn't so
much a word I link with a big deli sandwich, but alluring
certainly is. I suppose the foods themselves are pretty
dainty. If you hadn't guessed by now, this Latin word
gave us the modern adjective of delicate too. This is pretty
darn obvious, but somehow I had never noticed it. The
word delicate is within the word delicatessen!

PHARMACY

Another kind of shop, but this one sells medicine, which
is just as good as a deli sandwich, but in a different way.
This word applied to the actual medicines themselves
before being applied to the buildings that sell them.
Pharmacy is, unfortunately, one of those words where we
aren't sure exactly where it came from because medicine
and the study of how to heal the body is so ancient. We
can trace it all the way back to the Greek *pharmakon,*
which means not only "a drug" but can also mean "a
charm/spell/enchantment/poison." I guess these were
other ways people of the past thought they could cure
illnesses. I have also seen Greeks more succinctly use this
word for "remedy."

There is a theory that this Greek term dates back to the
even older ancient Egyptian word of *ph-ar-maki,* which
means "bestower of security." This name is thought to

be small, modest buildings in a cemetery or they can be feats of incredible architecture. India's beloved Taj Mahal is a mausoleum. Their association with death makes these buildings somewhat spooky, so much so that the word has become a term people use for all scary buildings in general.

The latter part of this name we see in other words too, most noticeably with museums. It was a word-forming element of Greek origins we use for buildings. The former part of this name is where things get interesting, as mausoleums are named after one person in particular—a man by the name of Mausolus, the ruler of Caria (a part of modern Turkey) from roughly 377 BC to 353 BC. He was a beloved and great ruler, most noticeably lending a hand in the ancient Greek War of the Allies; his involvement allowed the allied city-states to overcome Athens. Of course, his death was upsetting to many people, most noticeably, his widow (and sister) Artemisia. To mourn his death and celebrate his life, she helped direct the construction of a huge building that would house his dead body. This building would be named after him, a mausoleum. This initial mausoleum would go on to be known as the Mausoleum at Halicarnassus, a grand building considered to be one of the seven wonders of the ancient world. From this wonder, the word mausoleum was applied to all buildings that housed the remains of people.

BUNGALOW

We humans live in all kinds of buildings, from multiple-story homes to apartments in skyscrapers. Yet the kind of home with the most fun name (at least in my opinion) are bungalows. Bungalow is the name for a type of house that comprises just a single floor—ideal for those bored of stairs. Any kind of home, as long as it's over one floor, can be considered a bungalow, regardless of where it is in the world. This wasn't always the case, however, as initially bungalow was a word to denote a kind of house built in a way that was specific to the Indian subcontinent.

In India's east, Bengal is home to parts of the nation of India and the nation of Bangladesh. Traditional homes here are built across just one level. In Hindi, this kind of home became known as *bangla*, meaning "a low house in the Bengal style," and this Hindi word was adopted by the language of Gujarati, another local tongue. In Gujarati, the word became *bangalo*, meaning "a one-story house," regardless of if it was in Bengal or not. This Gujarati word eventually made its way into the English language, where it was corrupted into bungalow as we know it today, where it got applied to all one-story homes regardless of how Bengalese they are.

79

GROCETERIA

Let's wrap this chapter up with a building name that could have been. The shops where we buy our food are known collectively as supermarkets or grocery stores throughout the English-speaking world. The shops, however, could have gone by an entirely different name; in an alternate history, we may all be doing our food shopping in groceterias.

Supermarkets are pretty similar all across the globe. Shelves stacked with goods you compile yourself, which are then scanned through at checkout. This wasn't always how we bought food though. In the past, customers would walk into stores, tell the shopkeeper what they were after, and, in turn, the shopkeeper would collect and wrap up their goods for them. It was a slower experience but certainly has a charm to it. It was during the early years of the twentieth century when things started to change. Instead of clerks tending to customers' whims, the stock started to come packaged, and customers would pick them up from shelves. Cutting out the clerks meant saving money and time for the store owners. Stores like this started to appear more and more, with Piggly Wiggly (a name that I'd love to cover another time) being the first of its kind to open in the states in 1916.

This kind of store was so revolutionary that it needed a new name, and one that was trademarked a few years prior in 1913 was groceteria. It was hoped that this word would be used for these self-service supermarkets. What I enjoy so much about this name is how it's logical. The former part comes from grocery, of course, though, that latter part was inspired by the name cafeteria. The name "groceteria" was inspired by the name cafeteria because cafeterias are places where you serve yourself food. I guess the hope was that this -teria suffix would become the de facto for all things self-service, and while I read that groceteria did have some staying power through the 1920s, it's a name that ultimately got lost in time.

Occupations

Every occupation is important. Regardless of how much those who do it get paid, or what the ins and outs of that occupation even are. Once we started to develop into the humans we are today not everyone needed to be a hunter-gatherer. Different people could benefit the community in different ways and, in return for their good deeds, be financially rewarded. Thus, the concert of jobs was born. It might be a little more complex than that, but I am sure you get the idea. Many kinds of jobs have come and gone, and I am sure new kinds of occupations will arise in the future. Our world is forever changing, and we need people to occupy those changes. I will be covering occupations all across the spectrum because, as I stated at the top, all jobs are important.

FARMER

This one might seem a tad obvious. I am mentioning it first to cover ground on a lot of occupations. The name "Farmer" encapsulates the most recurring way in which we create names for occupations, and that's with the help of our good friend, the -er suffix. The -er suffix is what we use to change a verb into a noun. Verbs are, of course, words we use for actions, and most jobs revolve around one key action. With our farmer example, the verb that best encapsulates their job is farm, so add an -er to the end, and we have farmer. This is the way we create many occupation names; do you drive for a living? You're a driver. Do you clean for a living? You're a cleaner. Do you plumb for a living? You're a plumber. I could go on. This convention is always being used, and people get creative with it sometimes. A popular job in recent years is making

YouTube videos for a living. YouTube is a noun already, but that hasn't stopped people from adding -er to the end and creating YouTuber.

Obviously, farmers existed way before YouTubers, and while I intended on farmer being a title to introduce this section with, it turns out farmer and farm have a pretty interesting origin too. While we associate the occupation of farmers now with people who milk cows, grow crops, and drive tractors, this wasn't always the case. Farmer comes from the verb of farm of course, and this verb comes from Anglo-French roots with their word of *fermer*, initially meaning "to rent." Over the years, this Anglo-French word became farm but still meant "to rent," meaning a farmer was someone who collected rent. Someone who collects debts is different from someone who cultivates carrots, so how did the occupation title end up being applied to farmers as we know them today? In the sixteenth century, the land people grew crops on was often secured on a renting basis. So that verb of farm, meaning to rent, applied to the land as its name, and its noun form became the name of the people who worked this rented land, farmers.

Farming like this existed way before the sixteenth century, and in this time, farmers had different names. One I read of was "churl," which was an Old English word for "peasantry." However, another old name for farmers was "husbandmen." Husband comes from old roots meaning to care for something, and while we no longer call farmers "husbandmen," we still use the term husbandry when talking about looking after plants and animals, and of course married men are called husbands as traditionally they look after their married partner.

ATTORNEY

Lawyer is a pretty easy name to understand; it's molded from the same cloth as the aforementioned -er occupation names. Attorney, however, is a little different. Attorney and lawyer are terms that seem to be used interchangeably; however, there is something of a difference. Lawyer can be used as a title for anyone who gives legal advice as a career, while an attorney is a kind of lawyer who represents people in court. It also seems that "lawyer" is primarily an American term; here in the UK, we use the term "solicitor." Once again, solicitor comes from changing solicit into a noun; this time, we get an -or instead of an -er.

Despite being a primarily American term, "attorney" comes from French roots. Old French gave us the verb *atorner*, meaning "to assign," and this verb gave us the Old French job name of *atorné*, which eventually transformed into attorney. So the name can be seen as meaning "one who is appointed," as that's exactly what attorneys are—they are people appointed to help in legal situations. There are, of course, different types of attorneys too, from prosecutors to defense attorneys to family lawyers to barristers. However, the difference between all kinds of lawyers can be just as confusing as the law itself.

85

AUTHOR

An occupation I have the great pleasure of calling my own—well, as long as you guys keep buying these books anyway. While we may link this occupation most with those who write books, this word was used much more broadly in the past. In the fourteenth century, this word was instead *acteor*, and it meant someone "who makes or creates" without pointing to books specifically; you could create anything and be considered its author. That could still apply today. This word of *acteor* had an even broader meaning—"creator" or even "father."

It meant these things rooted all the way back to the Latin word of *auctor*, which could mean "promoter, producer, father, progenitor, founder, trustworthy writer, doer, or responsible person," (just to name a few). This word also, in a literal sense, apparently meant "one who causes growth." It's a word with a lot of meanings, that's for sure, and all these meanings relate to being the creator and having complete control and making things bigger. This is because its roots are the word-forming element of aug-, which means "to increase" and can be found in other words cross language. Perhaps most noticeably, authority, which explains why authority sounds similar to author, but meanings relate to other definitions of those Latin and Old French words. Most authors like to claim they are the authority on what they are writing, but that's not always the case; they'll let anyone write books these days!

DOCTOR

In the past, a lot of medical work was carried out by religious figures. We have all sorts of tales of monks performing operations and even amputating limbs. While in modern times, most of the world has a clear separation between churches and hospitals, the word doctor has roots in these religious origins. The medieval Latin word of *doctor* meant "religious teacher" and came from *docere*, meaning "to show/teach/know." Over time, doctors went from being used for religious teachers to high-level teachers in general. Studying anything in an official capacity for a long enough time allows you to earn the title of doctor. Despite this, the occupation is most heavily linked with the medical world as you have to be a doctor to be allowed to save human lives in this capacity.

While doctor is far removed from its religious roots, it can still be found somewhat in religion, like with the word of doctrine, for example. A doctrine is a set of beliefs followed by a religion. Doctrine comes from doctors as they both relate to teaching. Doctors and doctrines both teach people things. This, of course, created the term "indoctrinate," which is the opposite of teaching people and is instead forcing your beliefs on them.

LUMBERJACK

Many consider this to be one of the manliest professions on our planet, though that's a stereotype. In reality, anyone can be a lumberjack, regardless of their gender or sex. I guess the primary reason as to why people think this job is so manly is due to the use of the name Jack, which is more popularly a male name. Lumberjack is, of course, a combination of the terms lumber and jack. Why aren't they known as lumberdaves or lumbergrahams? This is because in the past jack was a catchall term for men in general; any man could be called a jack. It's why this name appears in other sayings like "jack of all trades."

Lumber is the name we use for chopped-up wood; considering this job revolves around chopping wood, it makes sense as to why it would be used in this occupation. What I like, however, is how we got this term of lumber for wood. Before being the name for chopped, "lumber" was and still is a verb meaning to move clumsily/awkwardly. As these huge planks of wood were awkward to move around, the verb "lumber" is thought to have been applied to them. So with lumber being a word for clumsy and jack being a word for men in general, this occupation title could be seen as meaning clumsy men, which isn't quite as manly now, is it?

As I mentioned, we are well beyond the point in which only men are allowed to chop down trees for a living. Should we be using this term for lumberjack for women too? Well, it's a debated subject. I have read that female tree-choppers can be called lumberjacks too; however, the term lumberjill has been thrown about too. I guess this derives from the nursery rhyme of Jack and Jill. I have also found some much more appropriate gender-neutral terms too, like logger or forester. Maybe the term lumberjack will come tumbling down like the trees someday.

CONCIERGE

This is, without doubt, a fancy-sounding occupation; it's the proper title of the hotel employee who assists guests with things such as dinner, theatre, and excursion bookings. If you're talking to a concierge, then there's no doubt you are about to have a fun time. The reason this occupation sounds so fancy to an English-speaking oaf like me is that this word is French, and French is always going to sound fancier than anything in English. I imagine this job wouldn't be held in the same regard if they were called hotel receptionists.

While concierge might seem like a posh word now, its origins definitely aren't as posh. I'm sure a lot of us feel like slaves at the worst of times during our workdays; for concierges, however, being a slave is quite literally in the job title! The "con" at the start means together, like with the word "connect." The latter part of the title is thought to come from the Latin *servius*, meaning "slave." So the occupation title is thought to mean "fellow slaves" or "slaves together," which isn't the most morale-boosting, that's for sure! I guess in a way this name is quite posh, as in the past posh people would have had slaves, and now they have concierges.

89

BEST BOY

If you spend a lot of your time watching the credits of a film like myself, perhaps in the hopes there'll be an after-credits scene, then there's no doubt you have seen this title pop up during that final scroll. Like me, you may wonder every time, "What on earth does a best boy do on a movie set?" Well, to understand what a best boy does, we need to understand what the gaffer and key grip do. The gaffer is the title held by the head of a film's electrical department, and a key grip is a title held by the head of the film's grip department ("grip" meaning behind-the-scenes rigs). Both the gaffer and the key grip have a second in command, the best boys.

How can they be the best if they're only second in command? Surely, you'd want your best boy to be top dog, right? Well, the story goes that in the past when gaffers and key grips would need a hand with something, they would say something like, "Get me the best boy for the job," and these "best boys for the job" earned that as a title for themselves. I know what you're wondering— yes, best boys can be girls too. I have read the term "best girl" can be used, as well as best person, for a gender-neutral title.

90

FISHMONGER

Fish is one of those words that doesn't have the most interesting of origins, since fish have been around forever. It's thought to ultimately go back to the proto-Indo-European with their word of *pisk*, which is similar to other languages' words for the creatures, like the Italian *pesce* or the Spanish *pez*. Ps and Fs switching across languages isn't too uncommon; think of the English "father" and the Latin *pater*. Anyway, that's off-topic; what you need to know is that "fish" is an old word not of the clearest of origins. So why have I chosen to cover it here? Well, because of the latter part of this occupation's name: monger.

A fishmonger is someone who prepares and sells fish, like a butcher but for underwater animals. The "monger" part of this name roots in the Latin words *mango/mongo*, which means "a dealer/trader." It has nothing to do with the fruit or the illustrious publishers. So fishmonger simply means "fish dealer." If this word means dealer, then why isn't it present in more occupation names? Why don't we call butchers meatmongers or grocers carrotmongers? Well, we may have in the past, but over the years, those other titles usurped them. Monger does live on in some other names however. Take an ironmonger, someone who trades iron and other metal goods, or even a warmonger, a person who deals in the brutal art of war. There are mongers all around us, though the fish type is most popular.

MATADOR

I wasn't too sure if this counted as a job at first; however, upon search, I read that top matadors get paid quite handsomely for their skills and are treated like rock stars, so I imagine to some this is, in fact, a full-time job. It's a controversial job at that too. For those unaware, a "matador" is a Spanish name for a "bullfighter." Bullfighting is a controversial performance due to how the bulls are treated and ultimately killed. The name for the people who do the killing doesn't try to sugarcoat this fact. Matador means "killer" in Spanish. It's the noun form of their verb for kill, *matar*. I have no doubts that this activity will remain under scrutiny for the foreseeable future, and the fact the title of the key performer means killer probably won't help those in favour of the tradition.

SHRINK

Psychologists and psychiatrists seem to have amassed an awful lot of nicknames over the years; undoubtedly, the most popular of all of these has to be the term "shrink." How on earth did a verb for making things smaller end up as a more jovial term for people who study the brain and its functions? This nickname for the occupation has origins in the native tribes of the Amazon rainforest. These tribes are known for preserving and shrinking down the heads of their enemies. These tribesmen were known as "headshrinkers," and this act of shrinking heads was seen as a mystical, magical process for shaymen to master.

At first, it was this complete term of headshrinker that was applied to psychotherapists; this is an allusion to the strange stuff that Amazonians did with heads. It's thought that the work psychotherapists did with brains and the head was similar to what the tribes did—well, at least similar enough to tease them with that name. It's thought that this term came about in the 1960s, and some specifically give author Thomas Pynchon credit with coining the term in 1966. Since then, however, this term originally meant to mock and compare psychologists to shaymen of the rainforest has been adopted by those in the role.

Websites

Whether you are clicking at them with a mouse on the computer screen or thumbing through them on your phone in a dedicated app, websites have quickly become one of the most prominent features in all our lives. We buy things through them, learn things through them, get our news from them—some of us even find our loved ones through them. While there are countless websites out there covering all sorts of niche interests, a handful of them have become juggernauts in our modern world. It's these huge omnipresent websites that I will be looking into here. Though you won't find the name of the most popular website here, Google, because I explained Google's name in the previous book, which you have obviously already read, right?

AMAZON

If you can think of it, Amazon will most likely sell it and ship it to your front door. You may well have purchased this book from Amazon, or you may be reading it on a device owned by Amazon or even listening to it through another website owned by Amazon. Amazon started selling books, and it was thanks to a certain book as to how the company got its name—that book being the dictionary.

Amazon went through a series of possible names before; most noticeably, it was cadabra.com, as in the thing magicians say. This was ditched, however, as many thought it sounded too much like cadaver. In search of a new name, Amazon's founder Jeff Bezos searched through the pages of a dictionary to find an answer. He wanted a name starting with A so they would appear first or near the top of various directories. It was in the pages of the dictionary where he found the name Amazon, and it spoke to him. Before being the name of the world's biggest store, it was the name of one of the world's biggest rivers. Bezos wanted to make a website that was unfathomably huge, so huge that the sheer size and magnitude of it would leave people in awe, much like the Amazon River. He got his way, as Amazon.com is now pretty darn big.

There were other ideas toyed with, including Awake, Browse, Bookmall, and Relentless. Some of these names got further than others. If you visit relentless.com to this day, you will still be directed to none other than Amazon.

REDDIT

The website Reddit often likes to bill itself as the front page of the internet, and that's for a good reason. Reddit is a link-sharing website as opposed to being a website that hosts content; it's a place where people share content from other websites. It's where an awful lot of things that become viral on the world wide web begin. This means that by being active on Reddit, you get a sneak peek as to what's going to become popular soon; it is the ground level for the internet. This means, however, when your friend or family member shows you an interesting picture or article, it's most likely that you have already seen it or read it on Reddit.

This is why the website has that name—it's a pun! After spending enough time on the website, when someone shares an interesting article or funny story with you, you'll most likely say to them, "Yeah, I already read it on Reddit." It was a presumptive thing to call the website in its early days, but sure enough, it proved to be the correct name to go with. The name also ties up pretty nicely with the Latin word of "reddit" too, which means "to submit for approval," which is fitting as Reddit is a website where people submit things in the hopes the internet approves of it. What a fun coincidence, and, yes, I read that tidbit on Reddit.

BAIDU

It should come as no surprise that I spend quite a lot of time on the internet, so how have I never visited the website of Baidu? It's ranked as the fourth most popular site on the entire internet, yet I have never heard anyone around me using it. Well, that's because this is a Chinese website, their de facto search engine. So while it's more or less unused outside the nation, China's massive population alone makes this one of the world's most popular sites. The name of this website has similar etymologies to Google's, its worldwide counterpart. Google comes from the number of a googol, which is a one followed by one hundred zeros. The search engine was named after this impossibly large number to represent the impossibly large number of results the search engine could provide.

Baidu's name is similar, as it literally translates to "a hundred times" or "countless times," which also evokes this image of a staggeringly huge amount of answers. What's especially interesting about this name is that it wasn't chosen to have a similar meaning to Google's name as the term comes from a line from the classical Chinese poem, "Green Jade Table in the Lantern Festival" by Xin Qiji. The line reads, "Having searched hundreds of times in the crowd, suddenly turning back, he is there in the dimmest candlelight." This shows us the name Baidu not only plays on the same concept as Google's name but is also a nod to the wonderful poetry from China's history.

INSTAGRAM

Those old enough may remember that Instagram's original logo was that of an old-fashioned instant camera; the spirit of these cameras is what inspired the app. The appeal is taking a photo and being able to share it straight away with everyone. It's from these instant cameras as to where the "insta" part of the name comes from. Yes, these kinds of cameras aren't called Polaroid cameras, that's just the name of the brand most known for making them. The latter part of the name also has roots in spontaneity and receiving things quickly, telegrams. Telegrams were the original instant messenger, a way in which brief messages could be sent around the world in a quicker amount of time. Once again, telegrams inspired the creators of Instagram and especially influenced the platform's name. Instagram's name is little more than a portmanteau of instant camera

97

and telegram. Two outdated technologies gave us the name of this modern website.

EBAY

There are few things more stressful online than the final seconds of an online auction, seeing that timer tick down and praying no one will outbid you on whatever you are trying to obtain. While they now do more traditional selling these days, eBay will always be best known for its auctions, and, yes, I do in fact have to spell it with the lowercase *e* and uppercase *b*—they're the rules. The site's original name reflected these auctions much more clearly, simply being called AuctionWeb. After the first successful sale on the website (infamously being a broken laser pointer), site founder Pierre Omidyar wanted to go with a unique name.

Omidyar initially wanted to name the site after his technology consulting firm, Echo Bay. Unfortunately, echobay.com was already taken by a mining company in Canada. So instead of calling it Echo Bay, he decided to shorten Echo to e and call the site eBay. A lot of people presume that the e stands for electronic, and while that is a logical idea, it isn't the case. What I couldn't find out, however, was why Pierre Omidyar named his firm Echo Bay in the first place. There are some places on our planet with that name, but I couldn't find any connection between these places and this man; maybe he liked the name.

ASK JEEVES

It might seem odd to imagine now, but there was a time when the internet was a new thing. While we can all more or less navigate the web with ease, at the start, people needed a helping hand with understanding how basic web browsing worked. You have to imagine how alien putting something into a search box and getting a result would have seemed in those early days. Luckily a certain someone was able to lend a helping hand in those early days—Jeeves.

Jeeves has been the quintessential butler name since the publication of the Jeeves and Wooster stories by P.G. Wodehouse in the early twentieth century. Butlers are seen as helpful people who can assist in any way possible; they are a good metaphor for search engines, especially at a time when people didn't quite understand search engines. This is why the name Jeeves was used in the name of the search engine of Ask Jeeves. This name was accompanied by an image of Jeeves himself, looking exactly how you'd imagine a butler named Jeeves to look. The use of the name Jeeves easily made people realise that they could ask this search engine a question the same way they could ask an actual butler named Jeeves. Ask Jeeves played a pivotal role in helping those early adopters of the internet understand exactly how the world wide web worked.

As the years went on and people came to grips with the internet, Jeeves wasn't as needed anymore. He wasn't made redundant; he had simply done his job. In 2006, the site's name was changed to simply Ask.com, and a blog

99

post was published explaining that Jeeves was retiring. While the name may not live on, his legacy certainly does. Incidentally, there's a chance that we shouldn't have ever had Ask Jeeves as a name in the first place, as the site's creator never got permission to use the name and likeness of Jeeves, the literary character, from the estate of P.G. Wodehouse.

YAHOO!

Another site from those early days of the internet. While there is one main Yahoo website, they have their fingers in many online pies, from Yahoo Maps, Yahoo Mail, Yahoo News, and the infamous Yahoo Answers. The fact that the website encompasses so much of the internet is why its original name was "Jerry and David's Guide to the World Wide Web," as it was something of a guide to all things internet. Those names of Jerry and David belong to the site's founders Jerry Yang and David Filo. They aren't random names.

As the site grew, it became apparent that it needed a less cumbersome name. Jerry and David decided on the word yahoo as their website's name. These two guys seem to have a pretty good sense of humor, as they claimed that Yahoo is an acronym for "Yet Another Hierarchical Officious Oracle," which is rather silly indeed. Though they have also said they chose the word as they like its informal meaning—slang for a rude, unsophisticated Southerner of the United States. This image of being the silly outsider of sorts appealed to them, and they have been Yahoo ever since. I ought to say they have been

Yahoo! ever since, as their name legally has to have the exclamation point in it because the name of Yahoo was already owned by a BBQ sauce company.

ROTTEN TOMATOES

In these modern times, people aren't fussed about how many stars movies get; instead, they want to hear that their film is certified fresh or dread to hear that the film they have been waiting years to see is considered rotten. Most importantly, people hope that their film gets a good score on the Tomato-meter. This new lexicon we use for film critique comes to us thanks to the movie review-aggregation website, Rotten Tomatoes. This name might seem incredibly odd for a website all about the quality of films and performances, but tomatoes and the quality of performances have a long-interlinked history.

Imagine Shakespeare's globe theatre, or any other suitable grand stage. On this stage is a performer of some kind—an actor, singer, dancer, whatever. Unfortunately, they aren't doing the best of jobs, and the audience are starting to realise this. What happens next? Well, we all know the classic image of a performer being booed off stage for being terrible; this is usually followed up by the hurling of rotten produce onto the stage. The practice of throwing vegetables at things you don't like is an age-old tradition. We have evidence of Roman Emperor Vespasian being so unpopular that he was pelted with turnips in the first century AD.

101

As the years went on, this act of throwing vegetables at things you don't approve of made its home in the theatres. Thanks to their shape, size, projectile-ness, and their satisfying splat, rotten tomatoes became the go-to produce to hurl at bad actors. The first recorded instance of this dates back to 1883, in which an actor was pelted with rotten eggs and rotten tomatoes in New York City. Rotten tomatoes for centuries have been associated with how people perceive performances they watch. Instead of displaying their distaste for films with actual rotten tomatoes these days, audiences now go to the website of Rotten Tomatoes to show their displeasure in film. It's an incredibly fitting name despite how odd it seems at first.

It wasn't due to this fact as to why the site has this name. The site's creator Senh Duong was a huge fan of the film *Leolo*, which involves a boy who imagines his parents are an Italian peasant and a giant tomato. The paternal tomato of this film helped inspire the name too. While not too many people have heard of this exact film, it played a huge role in cinematic history in helping name perhaps the most popular film-based website on the internet.

YOUTUBE

Despite its many flaws, it should come as no surprise that YouTube holds an incredibly special place in my heart. I wouldn't be writing this book if it were not for this website. YouTube now holds the title of the second-most visited website in the world, just behind its search engine owner. The site's name, however, is pretty straightforward. The "you" in the name represents well, you! This is because the website allows anyone to upload videos to the site. The "tube" part comes from an old nickname for televisions, the tube. Televisions were called tubes because older TVs were made up of things known as cathode-ray tubes. It's this tube that brought shows and movies to so many people in the past and why televisions are still known as the tube to some to this day.

While traditional television is undoubtedly still popular, YouTube has ushered in a new form of content for millions to watch and enjoy. In many ways, though, it's like traditional television, except instead of actors and performers being on the tube, it's ordinary people like me and you making videos in their bedrooms and basements. It's a tube for you.

THE ONION

The Onion likes to tout itself as America's finest news source. While the website is incredibly popular and its articles are read by many, those articles may not be exactly the truth. *The Onion* is a satirical news website dedicated to poking fun at modern affairs. This parody has become so popular that *The Onion* has spawned books, videos, and even a movie! Before all this, however, and even before the website itself, *The Onion* was a weekly satirical newspaper created by two college students in Wisconsin. There are two ideas as to why this paper was called *The Onion*. One is that it was supposed to mock the name of an actual newsletter from their college called *The Union*, which makes sense as onion and union are pretty similar words. Interestingly enough,

103

the actual word of onion relates to the word of union. The veg was named this as they are just one unified bulb, as opposed to garlic, which is made up of separate cloves.

The other idea comes from the creators' diets; they were so broke as students trying to make this parody newsletter that all they had for food was bread and onions. So the paper was named in honour of the onions they ate while trying to get their paper-turned-website up and running. Though like most things relating to the onion, maybe that's just a joke too.

Bands

I refuse to believe that there's no one reading this who hasn't at least once in their life wanted to be in a band, regardless of actual musical ability. There are those among us, however, that make that dream a reality and are living the life of a rock star! Or popstar? Or a hip-hop star? Musical bands come in many shapes and sizes. Undoubtedly, a key feature of a band is their name. Bands want a name that projects their image. It's why bands with names like Megadeth, Metallica, and Slayer all create heavy thrash metal music. You can tell by those band's names that their music isn't going to be smooth jazz, that's for sure. Their names, however, won't be covered in this chapter. Though the selection of band names I have chosen cross various genres and various levels of success.

THE BEATLES

Who would have thought that the name of an insect perhaps most closely associated with rolling balls of dung would become synonymous with the world's most popular band? Well, that isn't entirely the case, as the insect is spelt beetle, while the band is spelt "Beatles." Despite being one of the world's most talked-about and heavily researched bands, we aren't exactly sure how that name came about. There are all different ideas as to how they ended up with this name. It's worth noting that the band's original name was The Quarrymen, as when they started playing, John Lennon was at Quarry Bank High School.

Obviously, they didn't keep this name for too long, though; John Lennon was asked in an interview about the name and fed up with constantly being asked this question responded saying that in a dream, a man in a flaming pie appeared to him and said, "From this day on, you are Beatles with an A." While this answer comes straight from the source, most people can't help but feel Lennon was just a tad silly with his reply. A more realistic answer gives the band's former drummer Peter Sutcliffe the honour of coining the name, saying that the name "Beatles" was to play off Buddy Holly's minibeast-themed backing band The Crickets. For a while, they were the Silver Beatles; however, they dropped the silver in their name and went with just The Beatles.

But why the different spelling? Well, we aren't sure whose idea that was exactly, but regardless of who thought of it, we know why they thought of it—it's a pun. The Beatles made music, a.k.a. beats. That's why they went with that spelling of the name. It's pretty obvious, but I have met people who haven't realised this themselves.

107

THE KILLERS

No night out is complete without belting the lyrics to "Mr. Brightside" at one point. We have The Killers to thank for so many great rock hits. In the music industry, we now link these words with this band, but actual killers are pretty darn threatening! How on earth did such a beloved band end up with such a murderous name? Is it because they have some killer tracks? Well, not quite. They stole the name of another band. Well, kind of.

While now known primarily for rock songs, The Killers have always had a penchant for electronic/techno music too. Their earlier tracks were more electric than rocking. One of Brandon Flowers' (The Killers' front man) biggest inspirations is the rock/synth band New Order. New Order's 2001 single "Crystal" featured a fictitious band in its music video. Like a lot of bands, this fictitious band had their name across the bass drum, with that name being The Killers. Flowers loved New Order so much that he used the name of the fictional band in one of their music videos as the name of his real band. The Killers stole this name from another band that was using it. That other band just happens to not exist.

One last bit of name-based fun with this band is the name they use for their fanbase, the victims. This too seems like an odd name at first but makes an awful lot of sense and is rather clever when you remember what the band is called in the first place.

BLINK-182

Numbers can be names too, you know. It seems like an odd claim at first, but the band Blink-182 is a clear example of how this can be the case. Though why these numbers? And why blink exactly? Well, we don't seem to be too sure. Originally, the band was simply called Blink, though I haven't found a reason as to why they called themselves Blink—just a good name, I imagine. In fact, it's such a good band name that it was already taken. An Irish techno band was using the name Blink already and the band was told they would have to use a different name. Instead of thinking of a different name entirely, they slapped "182" to the end of their name and called it a day.

These numbers have caused quite an uproar over the years, though. People debate over what these numbers mean. The band insists they were randomly chosen, but they have also made up other stories for fun; most noticeably, the band's former front man claimed that 182 is the number of times Al Pacino says the F word in the movie *Scarface*. People have also debated how you say it. Is it "one eighty-two"? "One eight two"? "One hundred and eighty-two"? "Eighteen two"? That is another mystery revolving around this name.

DESTINY'S CHILD

109

The girl group with many great hits gave the world the megastar that is Beyoncé Knowles. Destiny's Child wasn't always their name, however; in the beginning, they had the far more generic name of Girls Tyme. I imagine this name came about simply because they were a female-centric band. Luckily, this name didn't stick around. Something I find so interesting about the name Destiny's Child is that possessive S. Who is Destiny? Who is her child? Why is the band named after this kid?

Well, Destiny isn't supposed to be anyone's actual name. Though I hope someone is a big enough fan of the band that they forced one of their parents to change their name to Destiny so they could literally be Destiny's child. Speaking of parents, this name came to be thanks to Beyoncé's mother, Tina Knowles. She supposedly suggested the name Destiny after seeing it in the Bible. The only issue was that they were unable to trademark the name Destiny. They still wanted to use that name but had to make it a tad more unique. This was when the word "child" came into the mix. I guess they could have just gone with Destiny Child, which is quite a provocative name unto itself. However, making it possessive gave the name more weight. Beyoncé has stated in an interview that the name "is like a rebirth of destiny," which is highly provocative too. The rebirth of destiny, the child of destiny, Destiny's Child.

DE LA SOUL

This hip-hop trio from New York state is anything but French, so how did they end up with a French name? Well, when translated into English, De La Soul simply means of the soul or from the soul. This is clearly how they think about their music, as being music from the soul. It's a lighthearted name for a band that makes such wonderful, light hip-hop. What's especially fun with this band, however, is how the three members chose their stage names. Posdnuos, Trugoy, and Maseo seem almost like gibberish at first. Though, in reality, these are just other words jumbled up and inverted. Posdnuos is "sop sound" reversed. "Sop Sound" was a name he used as a high school DJ. Trugoy is just yogurt spelt backward, as it's his favourite food. And Maseo is just an adaptation of his actual surname of Mason.

KRAFTWERK

Electronic instruments are a mainstay of the music industry now, though that wasn't always the case. The first band to have an entirely electric instrument lineup was the German techno band Kraftwerk. Their music, however, didn't sound like modern techno-pop songs. Their original music had a more industrial sound to it all. And it was this industrial sound that inspired their name.

German speakers will already know what exactly this name means, as *kraftwerk* is the German word for power station. Founding member of the band Ralf Hütter explained that when they first started recording music, there were electronics and tech all around them instead of traditional instruments. He felt that it didn't seem like a recording studio at all. But instead, it was more like a power plant. As Germans, they went with the German language word for these, hence why they are called Kraftwerk. I believe they have since gone on to perform in actual power stations; Kraftwerk in a *kraftwerk!*

111

THE POGUES

While most well-known for a certain Christmas song, The Pogues are a band with many great hits under their belt. While the band was formed in London and their lead singer was born in Kent, they have deep Celtic roots.

So much so that they are considered one of the biggest bands in the Celtic-punk genre of music. Unsurprisingly, this means that the band's name is from Celtic origins too, though Scottish-Gaelic, interestingly enough, not Irish-Gaelic, despite the band being so heavily linked with the Emerald Isles.

The band's original name was Pogue Mahone, which stuck from 1982 to 1984. Then someone asked them to change it, that someone being the BBC. As the band grew more popular, the BBC started playing more of their songs on their radio stations, which meant they had to say the band's name over and over live on air. What's wrong with that? I hear you saying. Well, the name Pogue Mahone is the anglicization of the Scottish-Gaelic phrase *póg mo thóin*, which means "kiss my arse." Those who spoke Scottish-Gaelic were outraged at having to hear this phrase constantly on the radio, so they complained to the BBC about it. This led to the BBC informing the band about these complaints and left them with a decision: keep the rude name but don't get played on the BBC or change it and get their songs played on the radio. Luckily, we know which option they took.

The part of the name they kept is the part that roughly translates to "kiss" in English, which means we have two bands with the name Kiss! Though I can't imagine you'd find The Pouge in black and white makeup and ridiculous outfits.

PARAMORE

The name of this band comes from quite an odd origin. Lead singer Hayley Williams has said that the band got this name as it was the maiden name of one of the band's former bass players. What a strange way to name a band. I can only imagine what names other bands would have if they were named after their former bass player's mother's maiden name. What's interesting about this band name is it's a homophone. Lovers of romance will be familiar with the word *paramour*, which is pronounced in the same way but spelt differently.

The word *paramour* comes from Old French origins from their words of *par* meaning "to/by" and *amour* meaning "love." In Old French, "to" was more an adjective/verb meaning to love someone. It got connected with a more sultry secretive kind of love, however, and when this word arrived in English, paramour was used more as a noun to mean a secret or illicit lover. The band didn't know of this meaning when they chose the maiden name as their band name but loved it. So the name was chosen as an ode to an old band member but due to its risqué connotations too. Upon looking into the last name of Paramore, it does seem to come from this French term. Perhaps the first to bear this name was someone's secret lover or even the offspring of a taboo relationship.

113

RUN THE JEWELS

Despite this hip-hop duo bringing the phrase "run the jewels" into the limelight in recent years, it's a phrase that predates the band. It's an old slang term for a "robbery, a stickup, a theft." I imagine it was initially linked with robbing a jewellery store where people would run (away with) the jewels. While I am not sure of the criminal records of the band's members and if they have ever "run the jewels," it doesn't seem to be the case that they are named after their love of stealing things. They were inspired to use the phrase as their name after hearing it in the song "Cheesy Rat Blues" by LL Cool J. The name was an ode to a song that made them fall in love with hip-hop in the first place.

What I read of interest about this name is that there was a film to be made in recent years that was going to be called *Run the Jewels*. The band Run the Jewels was unhappy with the film using the phrase as its name, however. It could be argued that Run the Jewels was angry that *Run the Jewels* was going to run the jewels with the term run the jewels!

BTS

Hailing from Korea, BTS quickly rose to fame as a worldwide sensation. Before you knew it, those three letters were appearing all over the place. Though what exactly do they stand for? Well, there are a few ideas. The name is an English initialism of the Korean phrase *bangtan sonyeondan*, which translates to "bulletproof boy scouts." While this might seem odd at first, this is quite a clever term. Boy scouts are traditionally young, and young people have a lot of expectations and stereotypes put on them. These issues facing young people are seen as bullets that could take you down. Being bulletproof, however, shows the world that you can deflect these issues. It was this overcoming of issues that faced the band that inspired the name.

More recently, the band confirmed that BTS would mean something else too—Behind the Scenes, which is what BTS has stood for historically. This wasn't just a silly corporate rebranding thing; it was supposed to reflect the level of attention bands get these days, thanks to things like social media. Now you can see so much more from a band, what they do on stage, or what they get up to behind the scenes.

Drinks

In the last book, I fed you heartily on food etymologies; however, I must have left you all rather parched, as I didn't cover the etymologies of any drinks. Well, this time around, let's make sure that all your thirsts are quenched by looking into how a variety of drinks got their names. Fluids are perhaps more important for our bodies to survive and can be just as tasty too. We'll be covering the common names for these drinks as well as some branded names too. Toward the end, we will even be looking into some alcoholic drinks, so make sure you have your ID ready when we get to that point.

WATER

Water is undoubtedly one of the single most important things for us and our planet. About 60 percent of the human body is made up of water, and around 70 percent of the planet is made up of water. It's the reason life has been able to flourish on this planet, and it separates us from all the other hunks of rock in the galaxy. When we explore the cosmos, we hope to find water because that could mean further life. Water is so gosh-darn important. It's a shame that its etymology isn't as fun. It's so vital to us that we have always had to have a word for it. And what we know about water is that it dates all the way back to the proto-Indo-European *wed,* meaning "water/wet." We aren't sure where it came from beyond this, but some think it may relate to another PIE word, *ap,* meaning "animate," as water was thought to be a living force that was animated. As I said, water doesn't have the most interesting etymology, but it's water, for goodness sake! I couldn't not mention it.

117

What I also find of interest with water are the other words used when describing it. Most noticeably, we have aqua and hydro. We used these words in lieu of water all the time, like with aquarium and hydroelectricity. Aqua simply comes from the Latin name for the stuff and hydro comes from Greek, the two languages that seemingly shaped so much of the world around us. These two words, aqua and hydro, both come from just as unknown origins as water.

MILK

Perhaps the second-most important drink—well, to us mammals at least. The milk produced by the bodies of humans and other mammals is the key feature that separates us from birds, reptiles, fish, and insects. In fact, the name mammal comes from the gland that produces milk, the mammary gland. Like water, this fluid's name is pretty ancient too, so it doesn't come from the clearest origins. Though luckily, it isn't as murky in origin.

Milk once again comes from PIE roots. With the PIE word of *melg,* which means "to wipe/rub/stoke." Why would milk be named after this word that seems fundamentally to be a verb? Well, it's because these are verbs that are strongly linked with milk. While we drink our mother's milk as children, as we grow, we drink the milk of other animals too—most noticeably cows. Though we don't drink the milk of cows in the same way we drink our mother's milk. Instead, we extract it out of them with a wiping/rubbing/stroking motion. This is why the word milk comes from this ancient verb, as it's how we acquire milk from animals. This is why milk/milking has become a verb too. We milk for milk! In Latin, the liquid was called *lac*, and that's why we use this word when talking about things that relate to milk, like lactose.

TEA

If you put together the fluids mentioned in the last two entries, boil it up, and add some leaves, then you have this wonderful drink: tea! Tea is considered the second-most widely drunk drink across the globe, just behind water. It's a drink that comes in all different varieties, whether that be herbal or even iced. While linked heavily with my home nation of the United Kingdom, tea's roots are in China. When first brewed in the far east, it was given the name of *tu*, which is represented with the Chinese character 荼. This name meant "bitter vegetable," as tea is somewhat bitter and made with plants. This Chinese name changed into *cha*, which is represented with the character 茶. These two Chinese characters are exactly the same minus one stroke. The scholar Lu Yu, who wrote a book about tea in 760 AD, gave it this new name by mistake when he forgot to add the aforementioned stroke.

This spelling mistake firmly entrenched the hot beverage with the name *chá*. Tea was brought over from China to Europe first by the Portuguese in the fourteenth century. In Portuguese, the word for the drink is still firmly *chá*. A hundred or so years after the Portuguese discovered tea, the Dutch started exporting it to Europe too. The Dutch stationed themselves in the Fujian province of China. The natives of this region pronounce the name of the drink rather differently; instead, they pronounce it as *thee,* which led the Dutch to use this name too. The Dutch brought the leaves to the shores of Great Britain, who instantly fell in love with the drink. This led to the English language adopting the Dutch name for the drink, which became tea. So the name tea is the English adaptation of the Dutch adaptation of the Fujian dialect adaptation of the Chinese name. A name that's just as interesting as tea's history in our world.

CAPPUCCINO

Maybe you aren't much of a tea drinker. A lot of the world is more obsessed with beans than leaves, with those being coffee beans. There are so many different kinds of coffees; honestly, this drink could have had a chapter unto itself. We will be looking into just one kind of coffee drink, the cappuccino, simply because its name has the best origin.

This means "little capuchin," so we need to ask ourselves what exactly is a normal-sized capuchin? This name refers to the capuchin monks, a specific order of monks best known for their attire which consists of long brown hooded robes. It's these robes that the coffee is named after. The coffee is named after these robes because the beverage is a similar colour to these robes: a rich brown. This is why some sources point out that cappuccino means hooded too, which it kind of does. I have read more tongue-in-cheek ideas about the name too. Some say the coffee is named after the monks as the classic bald patch on top of monks' heads reminded people of the milky foam on top of the coffee. Of course, there's also something else named after these monks too—capuchin monkeys. These monkeys are named after the monks much for the same reason as the coffee, due to the similar colours. Who would have thought that an order of monks, a type of coffee, and a species of monkey would all be connected by a name?

JUICE

Fruits and vegetables are marvelous things. Not only can we eat them, but we can also squeeze their liquids out and drink them! These liquids obtained from produce are called juice. Various juices have become staples of our lives like apple juice and orange, while some raise an eyebrow, like tomato and carrot juice. Creating a drink from produce is no new concept, as the name juice dates back over thousands of years. It came to English via the Old French *jus*, meaning "sap/liquid." This came from the Latin *ius*, meaning "broth." It's ultimately thought to come from the PIE *yeue*, meaning to "mix/blend," as that's what you do to fruit in the juice-making process. What I also find interesting about the word juice is how it's used to mean other things too; most noticeably, it's synonymous with electricity. Have you ever said, "My phone is out of juice"? While this seems like it must be quite a new thing, referring to electricity as juice isn't as new as you may think. We have evidence of the word juice being used in this light all the way back to 1896. This was before electricity was commonplace in people's homes. The link between the two was definitely made quickly.

COLA

More often than not, there's another word preceding cola; however, that's the name of just that one brand of cola drink. Many other companies produce cola drinks too. Coca-Cola blessed this type of carbonated drink with that word of cola, and Pepsi's full name is Pepsi-Cola. Coke definitely doesn't own the complete rights to the word as much as they'd want to. Before being the name of a sugary soft drink, cola was and still is the name of a seed called the kola nut. This seed and its tree are part of the cocoa family, and its main use is being added to soft drinks for flavouring. Cola drinks are simply named after the produce that flavours them, like lemonade or apple juice. Unfortunately, we don't know how exactly the kola nut got its name, other than it's from old West African roots.

What I am sure you noticed though is that the kola nut starts with a K, while the drink starts with a C. This wasn't an accident. Coca-Cola's inventor John Pemberton purposefully decided to use a C instead of a K in the name, as he felt two Cs would look nicer than a C followed by a K. Coca-Kola definitely doesn't look as nice.

DR. PEPPER

While not quite as popular, Dr. Pepper is one year older than Coca-Cola. Its creator, Charles Alderton, was a pharmacist and produced the drink while experimenting with different flavours and syrups on the soda fountain in his pharmacy. At first, like many carbonated drinks, it was marketed as a healthy drink that will help your brain. What you may have noticed is that its creator was a pharmacist, not a doctor, and his last name definitely wasn't Pepper. So how did this drink end up with this name? Was there a real Dr. Pepper?

Well, possibly. Dr. Pepper's official website likes to state that its creator named it after the father of a former lover of his. That's pretty strange, and there doesn't seem to be further evidence supporting this. Though that's the official word from the horse's mouth. If this is true, then we can presume that yes, there was a real Dr. Pepper. The other idea as to how this name came about was simply for branding reasons. The drink has a unique taste, which I suppose could be described as somewhat peppery. It's definitely got a kick to it compared to other drinks. The Dr. part could have been added to make it sound better for you. It was marketed as a health tonic to start with, and what's a better endorsement than having the title of doctor on your drink? If it's named after a doctor, it must be healthy for you, right? One thing we also know about this drink is its original name was Waco. It was called this because it was created in the town of Waco, Texas.

123

IRN-BRU

This drink is heavily linked with one particular nation: Scotland. Irn-Bru is heralded as the nation's national drink, and some sources claim that Scotland is the only country that doesn't have Coke as its most popular soft drink. While this drink is undoubtedly incredibly Scottish and has been produced in the land since 1901, it actually dates back to the United States. A chemical company sold a drink labelled IRONBREW in New York back in 1889. Like most soft drinks, it was first sold as a tonic to improve people's lives, hence why it was manufactured by a chemical company. Iron brew was meant to help with your strength, which explains why its logo is that of a strongman; it also explains the name to us. This brew will make you feel as strong as iron.

There was a slight issue with this name. It wasn't made from iron, and it wasn't actually brewed. This became a much larger issue in 1946 when new laws were put in place saying that product names had to be literally true to the product itself. This meant that Iron Brew had to change their name. This is why on modern cans of the orange stuff, you will find the name omits the vowels, as this was legally different enough for them to bypass this law and practically keep their original name. This regulation has since fallen out of fashion as off-brand versions of the drink are called Iron Brew. If it has no vowels, you're drinking the real stuff.

SPIRIT

Spirit is a word that has a lot of meaning, it can be used as the name of a ghost or haunted being, or it can be used as the name of something that can be lost in hard times. In the world of drinks, a spirit is something else entirely; spirit is used as the name of strong alcohols like vodka, gin, tequila, and whisky. Some spirits are so strong that instead of drinking them, we use them in industrial circumstances only. They are also sometimes known as liquors too, though this word just comes from the Latin word for liquid, *liqueur*. How on earth did these drinks end up having the word spirit applied to them?

There are a few ideas as to how the booze ended up with this name. One of the more popular theories gives Aristotle the credit of coining this name. He felt that drinking this strong alcohol put spirits into the body of the drinker. I'm sure a lot of us have had quite high spirits after indulging in some spirits, only to have them come crashing down the morning after. Another idea relates to the Bible and the Holy Spirit from the scripture. In Acts 2:13 of the New Testament, it is written that "the effects of the Holy Spirit on the disciples as intoxication from too much new wine." This is basically implying that being by the holy spirit is much like being drunk, hence why spirits are named after this specific spirit.

One last idea is that spirits are what ancient Arabic alchemists used for the vapour that rose off of liquids as they distilled them for their elixirs. What I find so interesting about this is that this isn't a case of two different words with different meanings sounding similar; the drinking kind of spirits were named after the supernatural kind of spirits.

COCKTAIL

A cocktail isn't one specific drink, rather a collective name for drinks made by combining other drinks. Cocktails' use goes beyond the world of drinks; anything that is a mixture of things can be called a cocktail. And obviously there are actual cocktails too, the tails of roosters. Is there a connection between these tail feathers and the drink? Well, the name doesn't relate to cockerels, but a different farm animal, horses. Before we had cocktails, we had cock-tailed. This was a term used for horses that had their tails clipped short. This shortening of the tail was to denote the fact that they weren't thoroughbred horses. Pretty soon, cock-tailed came to mean any horse of impure mixed breed; we can see from here how exactly a term for a horse created by mixing different horses came to be applied to a drink created by mixing other drinks. Especially as drinking alcohol and watching horses race often happen at the same time. This is just one idea as to how they got their name.

To begin with, there was only one specific mixture of drinks that could be called a cocktail, but as different concoctions were born, this term of cocktail got applied to all of them; that original mixture was the old-fashioned kind of cocktail, hence why we call it an old fashioned to this day. Beyond this, other kinds of cocktail names are ridiculous. We have the Cosmopolitan, named after how modern and cosmopolitan the drink was when first mixed in 1975. Woo Woos are thought to be named after the chant bartenders would make at a New York Mets game every time they hit a run. And Sex on the Beach was a name given to the cocktail as the guy who created them thought that sex on the beach was a favourite pastime for those who would enjoy the drink. Not all cocktails include alcohol. In recent years, nonalcoholic cocktails have become popular; these have a name unto themselves too—the cleverly crafted word of mocktails, or mock cocktails.

Colours

How dull would our world be without colours? From the blue in the sky and sea to the green of nature. Bright, wonderful colours make our world so unique. While colours pretty much outdate everything mentioned in this book, it would be hard to talk about colours if they didn't have names. So while these colours were around before us, it was humans that named them. I'm going to cover a mixture of colours here, from the most well-known colours to some of the more unknown, with names you'd only find on tins and tubes of paint.

RED

Coincidentally, I'm wearing a bright red jumper as I am writing these words. While my outfit for today had no bearing on my choice of colour, it is a testament to just how popular the colour is. It's one of the most eye-catching colours and is associated with things from lust and love to anger and destruction. In nature, red can be found most commonly in fire, in flowers, and in us. Red is the colour of our blood, and while we see this when we bleed, blood can also make us appear red without us having to be cut open. Most noticeably, blood for a variety of reasons can make our faces turn red. It was red faces that helped form the word red.

The name red dates all the way back to the proto-Indo-European *reudh,* which means not only red but specifically, ruddy. Ruddy is an adjective we use to describe someone with a healthy red face. Eventually, this PIE word split into ruddy and read. In Old English, this is how we spelt the name of the colour. Eventually, it was shortened in Middle English to just red. What's of interest is that the popular last name of Read is a remnant of Old English, as it means red. However, this colour and surname have nothing to do with the thing you are doing right now.

YELLOW

Yellow is an interesting colour. It has a huge variety of meanings; some link the colour with fear and cowardness, while many link it with happiness and glee. It helps that the little smiley faces we send to one another on an alarming basis are yellow, doesn't it? For me, that has solidified yellow's image as a joyful colour. Yellow is also linked with *The Simpsons* and LEGOs due to the skin tone used by characters from these worlds, both of which bring me great joy too.

The word yellow is seemingly inspired by one of the most joyful things in our universe, the sun! Yellow stems all the way back to the proto-Indo-European word of *ghel,* which meant "to shine." While a lot of things are able to shine, I have no doubts that this shining is related to the sun's shine. This means that the colour yellow is named after that big shining yellow ball in the sky that gives us heat, light, and life. This PIE word of *ghel* changed throughout its history. It eventually became *geolu* in Old English.

129

Now obviously, this name is noticeably different from our modern word of yellow in a lot of ways, but the most noticeable thing about it to me is the fact it starts with a G. How did we go from spelling this word with a G to spelling it with a Y? Well *geolu*/yellow is not the only incident of a G becoming a Y in the transition of Old English to modern English. For example, the Old English word for day was *dæg*. This shift in the language came about as English grew and shifted away from its Germanic roots, perhaps inspired by the Normans and their language in 1066. As other Germanic languages still maintain a G where English may use a Y. Like the modern Dutch word for day, *dag*. This is all a slight tangent from the word yellow but interesting nonetheless.

BLUE

Rounding out the primary colours in blue. This is a colour linked with calm, peace, and serenity. Despite being so different from the colour yellow, at least by our standards anyway, blue and yellow both come from surprisingly similar origins. Blue comes from the PIE *bhel*, which also

means things like "to shine/flash/burn." What on earth (quite literally on earth in this case) is blue and shining? Well, for me, one thing comes to mind in particular: the glistening, shining sea.

The sun and the sea are two different things, yet by the same means as the sun's shine gave us the word yellow, the sun shining onto the ocean, and, in turn, making that shine, may have given us the original word for blue. That's my idea on the matter. The sea is incredibly blue and shining, so it makes an awful lot of sense. The sky is also a shade of blue too, and as the sun is shining in the sky, perhaps this word comes from the blue of the sky. We just don't seem to be too sure. What we seem pretty confident about, however, is how connected these colour names can be at times. Some sources point out that the old word for blue also meant blonde. As we continue our quest for colour names, you will notice more of them come from similar roots too. Unlike yellow, blue didn't change as radically from Old to modern English. In Old English, it was simply *bleu*—the exact same letters, just mixed up.

GREEN

Viewers of my YouTube channel *Name Explain* will know that green holds a special place in my heart, as 99 percent of the time on the channel, my cartoon counterpart is draped in the colour. Green is perhaps the colour most often found in nature, and it's the colour linked with all things natural. The name of this colour comes from its natural roots. Green stems all the way to the proto-Indo-European *ghre*, meaning "to grow." What's great about this PIE word is it's not only the source of the word green but also the source of two other words, grow and grass. This makes all the sense in the world as these three things are interconnected. Green grass grows! This PIE word evolved into *grene* in Old English. This not only represented the colour green but also meant young and immature. This is understandable, as we link green with youth and new things growing. Oddly enough, this meaning for the word green still kind of exists today in the most unexpected of places. Professional wrestlers who are still new, young, and immature are called green. Clearly, the three favourite things of every pro wrestler are headlocks, suplexes, and referencing Old English words.

131

ORANGE

What was called orange first? The colour or the fruit? Well, thankfully, unlike the chicken and the egg, this one has a definitive answer. This came as a shock to me, but it was the fruit that bore this name first. The colour was simply named after the fruit. So how did the fruit get its name then? Well, we don't know the fruit's ultimate origins. What we do know is that the oldest name is the Sanskrit *naranga-s,* and with this word, we can trace it through history and see it become orange in English. From Sanskrit, it became *narang* in Persian, which became *arancia* in Italian, which became *orenge* in Old French (quite a leap, I know) before settling as orange in English.

The fruit made its way to the shores of Britain in the early sixteenth century. So enamoured by its bright shade, which was so rarely seen in Britain, the people of English's past decided to use the fruit's name for that colour in general. And yes, I know what you're thinking. What about carrots? British people must have seen them, and they're orange. Well, while that's true now, but in the past carrots were more commonly purple and white than orange. Also, pumpkins hadn't arrived from the Americas yet.

Anyway, this is the colours section of the book, not the fruit and vegetable section. The colour orange was present in Britain before the arrival of the fruit—in fires and certain flowers most noticeably. It wasn't present enough to justify making a whole new name for it. So what did they call the colour before the arrival of the fruit?

Well, they simply dubbed it *geoluhread* in Old English. If you have been following this section well enough, then you will know exactly what this name means. It's simply the old English words for yellow and red put together, as orange is just a combination of yellow and red.

PURPLE

Purple is a colour that doesn't appear too much in nature. This meant that when we were able to harness it as a dye, it was saved for only the most important of people, like kings and queens. This is why purple is linked to all things royal and regal. One of the intense ways in which we obtained the colour purple to us as a dye was by (and I'm not making this up) extracting mucus from the glands of a specific kind of shellfish, a species of sea snail we now call the murex. In the past, in Latin, it was known as the *purpura*. Why it was called this and this word's etymology, we aren't too sure about unfortunately. However, the name for this snail became linked with the dye its glands produced. This eventually led to the unique colour of this dye being blessed with this name too. As we have seen many times now, over the years, this word journeyed through languages until it reached Old English, where it became *purpul,* before settling on the spelling of purple we have today.

133

MAGENTA

Didn't I just cover this colour? Well, kind of. Magenta is a debated colour. Magenta is a specific shade of purple/

red but, what shade is magenta exactly, we don't seem to agree on. Whatever colour you have in mind when you think of magenta, let's go with that one. This colour's name comes from an incredible unique origin. In the region of Lombardy in northern Italy, you will find a small sleepy town. This town's name is unique, as it's called Magenta. It's believed that this town was somehow named after the Roman emperor Marcus Aurelius Valerius. I can see Marcus morphing into Magenta over a few thousand years.

How did this town end up lending its name to a shade of purple/red? Well, we have a battle to thank for that. A battle fittingly called the Battle of Magenta. This battle took place on June 4, 1859, in this town. It pitted the Kingdom of Sardinia and the French Empire against the Austrian Empire. After around a collective 15,000 casualties, Sardinia and France were victorious. Supposedly, a troop of French soldiers had a uniform that was a unique shade of purple. In celebration of this victory, the unique colour of this uniform was named after the town/battle, cementing magenta as the name of this colour. Never would I have expected a colour to be named after a battle!

OCHRE

Like magenta, ochre is a name that can be applied to a wide spectrum of colours, from yellows and oranges to a deep brown. It's a wonderful natural earthy colour. It makes a lot of sense as to why this colour would be so earthy, as before we could so easily synthetically create colours, ochre pigments and dyes were created from the earth. We get ochre pigments through a mixture of ferric oxide and various amounts of clay and/or sand. These things mixing together in the ground give us this wonderful hue. This is why ochre is not only used as the name for the colour itself, regardless of what it's on, but also used as the name for the soil that makes the colour. To answer this one, we need to find out how exactly this soil got its name.

Well, unfortunately, we don't seem to be too sure as to where this word comes from. We can trace it all the way to what the ancient Greeks called it, that being *khros*, but how they got that word, we aren't too sure. What we do know about this Greek name is that it meant pale yellow, which is quite removed from the shades ochre is applied to these days. Ochre today does come in a variety of colours, from browns to oranges to golds. Some of these unique shades of ochre have unique names. A great example of this is the colour sinopia, which is a reddish shade of ochre. The pigments that created this shade were first discovered in modern-day Turkey, and they were exported across the Mediterranean via the port town of Sinope, which resides in modern-day Turkey too. This wonderful colour came from this port town it was named after.

135

MAGNOLIA

Magnolia is one of those many dull shades of white that the paint industry has created. They try to convince us it is different from eggshell, ivory, sea salt, and all those other shades in the hope of selling us more paint. Okay, so that might be a tad hyperbolical. I will admit that yes, these are somewhat different colours, but I still think the paint industry is trying to fleece us all. White is one of those words that doesn't have the most interesting of origins; magnolia, on the other hand, does. Magnolia was initially not the name of a shade of white but the name of something that was this particular shade of white. With that thing being the flowers called magnolias, I guess I could have covered this one a few sections back.

The plant magnolia comes from a unique root. Its name doesn't derive from old Latin or Greek roots. In fact, this flower was named after someone. Charles Plumier was a French botanist, and he named this flower after another French botanist, Pierre Magnol. Why did Pierre deserve to have a flower named after him? Well, Magnol was the botanist who created the framework and structure in which we name plants and their species. He was the guy who first suggested that plant names should end with -ia, as many do to this day. It was only fitting that his own last name would be turned into a flower's name with -ia attached to the end of it. This means that this colour is named after a flower, which is named after a human.

SMARAGDINE

It's highly unlikely that there's a colour you haven't ever seen before. It's much more likely that there's a name of a shade that you have never heard of. If you're anything like me, smaragdine may be exactly that. If you were to look up this colour name, you wouldn't come across some bizarre colour you have never seen before. Instead, what you would find is a wonderful emerald shade of green. Smaragdine is basically just that, a fancy, fun-to-say version of emerald green. This comes from an old word for the gemstone; in Greek, emeralds are called *smaragdos*, which ultimately came from the Semitic *baraq*, meaning shine. This Greek word via other languages like Latin and Old French morphed into "emerald" in English as we have it today. While we may use emerald as the name of the gem, smaragdine is far superior as a name compared to just emerald green; this name simply translates into meaning emerald-like or emerald-coloured.

Body Parts

I am sure you know about all your vital organs and bones, but what about your jugular? Or even your anatomical snuffbox? There's a high chance that you don't know your body as well as you think. Luckily for you, this section of the book is going to cover how various parts of the human body, from the well-known to the obscure, got their names. Before we look into specifics, I want to highlight the word "organ." This word ultimately means "something that does a specific thing," which makes sense for our body parts. In the past, other words could be attached to the term organ to specify things. Instruments were a prime example of this, hence why harmonicas were/are also known as mouth organs. We also have pipe organs; their name has been shortened over the years to just organs. Hence how the big piano-looking thing in a church and the fleshy chunks in your body have the same name!

MUSCLE

The human body is thought to be made up of almost six hundred muscles. They are instrumental in our existence and are most closely linked with our strength. Despite being linked with strong people, muscles are named after a type of animal we don't link with strength by any means. In Latin, muscles were called *musculus*. This Latin name translates in English to mean "little mouse." As I said, teeny tiny mice are not the first animal to spring to mind when we think of strength.

How have these vital body parts become named after rodents? Well, it has nothing to do with the strength of mice, that's for sure. It all comes from the way muscles move under our skin, especially the bicep muscles. Ancient Romans felt that the movement made by muscles when they were being flexed looked like little mice running under the skin. The idea of mice running around under the skin isn't the nicest idea. But it went into the creation of a word beloved by bodybuilders and gym junkies alike.

The Romans were fond of little mice, as it wasn't just our flesh that was named after them. Another animal was named after them too, the shellfish mussels, albeit the spelling is a little different. We aren't as sure why the Romans named these mollusks mussels, but one idea is that it had to do with their shape. Perhaps their open shells reminded Romans of the ears of a mouse.

SKELETON

Skeletons are associated with all things scary and spooky, but they are, in fact, rather remarkable things. They're foundations of our body that hold everything that makes us who we are in place. If you want an idea of what we would look like without our bones, then imagine a slug, as they lack a skeleton. What's strange is that (unless something terrible happens) we don't ever get to see our own skeletons. This was especially the case in ancient times when x-rays didn't exist.

The most common way in which people would have seen a skeleton in the past is when the remains of someone or something were left to decompose after death. While many animals are left to become skeletons in the open, we humans tend to bury our dead. This would lead to skeletons being unearthed, and by this time a skeleton would be dried up. It's from this dryness as to where the skeleton gets its name. It derives from the Greek *skeletos*, meaning "dried up." These dry bones led to the name of our internal structure. Though, in reality, our skeletons are wet most of the time, at least while we are using them, anyway.

LUNG

This organ comes in a pair, and they allow us to breathe. They are undoubtedly important, though despite all the heavy lifting they do, their name is not quite as heavy. The name for this body part comes from the Old High German *lungun*, meaning the "light organ," with this name deriving from the proto-Indo-European *legwh*, meaning "not heavy/having little weight." This airy organ has an airy name indeed. The average adult set of lungs weighs about one kilogram, which isn't all that light.

141

Its actual weight in no way means that it's the lightest body part, so why is it named after this feat? Well, one idea is that this name comes from the culinary world. People enjoy eating organs; livers and hearts from various animals are common food around the world. While lungs aren't as commonly eaten, they still are. One source I read said that when all these organs are tossed into a boiling pot, they will all sink to the bottom minus one. Those being the lungs. The lungs could have gotten their name due to the fact they are far more buoyant in a cooking pot compared to other organs, though I haven't tested this out to see if it's true.

INTESTINE

Two organs in our body are given this name, the small intestine and the large intestine. These two organs work in tandem, helping our bodies process the food and fluids that we put into them. I'm sure you don't need me to explain why one is called small and why one is called large. The word intestine itself comes from the Latin adjective of *intestinus*, meaning things like "inward/ inside," simply because these organs are inside of us. I guess every organ could have this name. This also explains to us why sometimes intestines are used as a catchall term for body parts.

What I like about these organs are the names applied to them in English's past. Instead of being large and small, the intestines were described as *gross* and *subtle* in Middle English, respectively. These are still words that have connotations with large and small, though they have since gone on to acquire other meanings too. In Old English, the intestines as a whole were called *hropp*, which simply means "rope." If you have any idea as to what intestines look like, it will become clear to you as to why they were called ropes.

ELBOW

Bow is a word that has been linked with bending for
a long time now. A bow in a bow and arrow has to be
bent far back; if something starts to bend upon taking
on too much weight, we say it's starting to bow. And
even the act of bowing is when we bend ourselves over.
Our elbows do an awful lot of bending too. Hence why
they have this word applied to them. As for the el of our
elbows, well, this comes from the proto-Indo-European
word of *elina*, which means "arm." So the name roughly
means the bend of the arm, which is incredibly fitting.

JUGULAR

Who knew that specific veins had names? I imagine
jugular is perhaps one of the best-known specific vein
names. Our jugular veins run from our brains down our
throats to the heart. Their job is to take blood from the
head back to the heart. The Romans called this vein the
iugulum, which meant the "collarbone/throat." This name
goes back to the Latin *iugum*, which means "yoke." This
kind of yoke has nothing to do with the yolk of an egg.
Instead, it's the name for a contraption used to hold two
animals together. Most noticeably, two bulls would be
attached to a yoke when pulling a plow. The collarbones
do look somewhat like a yoke, so I imagine that's why
this name got applied to the shoulder area before being
localised to the throat and then these veins. You may
have noticed that those old Latin names for this body part
start with an I and not a J. This is because of the strange

143

history the letter J has. In Roman times, J was a variation of the letter I. It wasn't until the sixteenth century that the letter got the name and sound we link with it to this day.

What's also interesting about the jugular is the role this body part plays in a certain phrase, "Go for the jugular." We yell at someone to go for the jugular when we want them to defeat someone in a cruel, brutal manner. Whether they literally defeat someone in a fight or more metaphorically in an argument, we say this as the jugular is seen as a weak spot in the human body. A simple slash of the jugular would end the lives of most people. It's not the most pleasant image. But sometimes, we need to be vicious with our language, and this phrase and body part are clear reminders of that.

—
SPHINCTER
—

While we link this part of the body mostly with our bottoms, we have sixty different types of sphincters in our bodies. This is because a sphincter is a name we apply to any circular muscle that constricts to help regular the passage of various things through our body. Our bile ducts are controlled by sphincters; we have many around our stomachs, and even our eyes have sphincters in and around them. What I'm trying to say is that basically, your body is covered in butt holes, but so is everyone else's, so don't feel too worried about it.

The Greek word *sphinkter* was used to mean any sort of "band or lace" that could be bound or squeezed tightly. It was the Greek physician of Galen who applied this word to these body parts, as he noticed that the key thing sphincters did was squeeze tightly. Galen is a hugely important figure in the history of medicine; he also clearly happened to coin the word we use for our butts too.

PHILTRUM

Every part of your body has a name; you may just not be aware of what exactly that name is. Take the philtrum, for example. There's a pretty high chance you may have never heard of this thing, yet you see it every time you look into the mirror as "philtrum" is a proper scientific name for the groove of skin that lives between your nose and your upper lip. It's not just us that have philtrums either; many other mammals like dogs and cats have them too. Despite its presence on the face of all humans, primates, and many other mammals, it doesn't serve much of a purpose, at least for us humans, anyway.

While it may have no biological purpose, we humans have given the philtrum meaning, as it's seen as a rather intimate part of the body, most likely due to how close it is to the lips, a part of the body we have deemed incredibly alluring thanks to kissing. It's from this lovey-dovey connotation as to how the philtrum got its name too, coming from Greek, meaning "love charm." This is because we hope to charm those that we love with our mouths...and our philtrums? We have seen some romantic mythology in our mouths too, as the philtrum together with the top lip is sometimes called Cupid's bow. Our top lips and philtrums look somewhat like the famous bow and arrows belonging to the god of love.

145

ANATOMICAL SNUFFBOX

I promise you that not only is this a name used for a body part, but also, from what I can tell, it is the most official correct name for this body part. There's a lot to unpack with this one. What's a snuffbox? What makes this one anatomical? Where even is it? The anatomical snuffbox can be found on your hand—the area between the bottom of your thumb and the top of your wrist, to be exact. You'll notice that your hand deepens here a little; in some people, it sinks in more than others, so yours may be quite dramatic or not too noticeable at all. It's the fact that this area gets deeper as to why it has this strange name.

To understand what a snuffbox is, we first have to understand what exactly snuff is. "Snuff" is a type of tobacco; however, unlike the many other forms tobacco takes, snuff isn't smoked like a cigarette or pipe. Instead, snuff is a somewhat powdery substance that you inhale by sniffing up your nose. The name snuff unto itself comes from a corruption of sniff. Snuff tends to be sold in a small tin, a snuffbox. However, partakers of snuff by and large don't simply shove their nose in this tin and huff away. Instead, they normally take a small amount of the substance and place it on their hand, specifically the part of the hand that we now call the anatomical snuffbox. This sunken portion of the handmade snuff feels completely at home before it was ingested into the nostrils of its patron. This small groove in the hand was the human body's own snuffbox, which explains why it was referred to as anatomical, an adjective meaning relating to the human body.

PARTS OF THE BRAIN

Your brain is you. Yes, I know your bones and skin and other organs play a pretty vital role in making you tick along. But the defining features that differentiate you from all other humans can be found in the brain. Your thoughts, ideas, beliefs, interests, and disinterests are all held within the roughly three pounds of fleshy wrinkly substance hiding behind your eyes. The brain is a deeply complex thing, so complex that it's split into a variety of different sections, each with its own name. There could be a whole chapter of this book dedicated to parts of the brain, but for now, let's highlight a couple of them.

The cerebral cortex is the name given to the layer of tissue that covers the whole brain. While the name for this sounds like it's come straight from the pages of a comic book or from some mad scientist, it dates back to the Romans. The former part of the name comes from the Latin word for brain, *cerebrum*. The cortex part is Latin too, being the Latin word for bark, rind, shell, or husk. What's interesting is that the word cortex is applied to the outermost layer of all organs. We have stomach and liver cortexes too. This means that this fancy-sounding name of cerebral cortex simply means brain shell, which isn't as fancy-sounding.

Many parts of our brain are referred to as lobes; this is an old word with unknown origins. It's not only our brains

147

that have lobes though, as we have lobes all across our body—most noticeably our earlobes. The lobes of our brain have unique names, one being the temporal lobe. This is that part of the brain that is believed to deal with memories, specifically long-term memories. To understand memories, we have to understand time too, hence why this lobe's name features the Latin adjective for time, *temporal*. Not everywhere in the brain has a fancy Latin name; the Broca's Area is named after the person who studied it, Pierre Paul Broca. I mention this part of the brain as it's of huge interest to lovers of names and words, as this is the part of the brain where language is thought to be processed.

Though perhaps the most strange-sounding part of the brain has to be the medulla oblongata, the part of the brain that connects it to the rest of the body. As well as connecting everything, it's believed to control things like our heart rate, breathing, and blood pressure. So it's pretty darn important. The word medulla comes from the Latin *medius*, meaning "middle," as the spinal cord it's attached to runs down the middle of our bodies. The oblongata part of this name refers to the fact that it is oblong shaped. So this strange-sounding name could be simply explained as meaning oblong in the middle.

Despite all these interesting names, the actual name of the brain itself isn't too noteworthy. It evolved over time from older Germanic words into what we have today. What is impressive is that the brain created this name for the brain itself, making the brain the only thing in existence to have named itself.

Elements

I am hoping for a huge reaction from you all when I go through these names periodically. Okay, so now that I have those puns out of my system, we can properly begin this chapter. All matter is made up of elements, though I am not talking about the classic idea of elements such as earth, water, fire, and so on. Instead, I am talking about the chemical elements, the building blocks of our world that all neatly fit into the periodic table plastered on the walls of science classrooms across the globe. Some elements we have known about before we had an understanding of what exactly elements were. Others have only been added in recent years. I am going to try and cover a good mixture from the ones you all know and are vital to our existence to some elements that you have to delve a little deeper into the table to uncover.

OXYGEN

Oxygen has the honour of being the third most abundant element in the Milky Way galaxy. Oxygen's most important use for us is one of the key ingredients in the air that we breathe, so it's pretty darn important. The latter half of this name appears in multiple element names. It is simply an old Greek word meaning "to create/form." The first part of this name, oxy, is Greek too. In Greek, *oxys* means "acid." This means we can deduce that oxygen means acid-forming. Why? Oxygen is the element we link with fresh air, not acid. This is because early chemists thought that to create any sort of acid, oxygen had to be used, and while we know this isn't the case, that name has certainly stuck around.

The Greek word of *oxys* means more than just "acid," it also means "sharp." I guess acids are pretty sharp in some ways. It's from this meaning that we see oxy in other words too—most noticeably with oxymoron, the name applied to contradictory terms like bittersweet and living dead. In this case, moron still means exactly what you think it means, whereas oxy means "pointed/sharp." So oxymoron is seen as meaning sharp fool, which is something of an oxymoron unto itself, as sharp can also mean quick-witted, something morons do not tend to be.

HELIUM

This is another hugely abundant element in our solar system. It has many important uses and is vital for our existence. Despite its mighty importance, most people know it for two simple reasons. It's the gas we put in balloons, and more importantly, it makes our voices go high when inhaled. These jovial uses for the element give helium a silly image, that's for sure. The element is heavily linked with the sun because our nearest star creates a huge amount of helium, and trust me when I say huge. The sun generates almost 600 million tons of helium every second. That would fill quite a few balloons. Helium was also first detected in the sun.

151

It is because of all these ties to the sun as to why the element is named after that life-giving ball of gas we all depend on. The name helium derives from the Greek name for the sun, *helios*. The sun wasn't the only thing that the Greeks named *helios*, as it was this exact name that they gave to their god of the sun too. The element could be seen as being named after a Greek god just as much as it's seen as being named after the all-important sun. So next time you're playing with helium and using it to make your voice go high, remember that you are sucking on the gas of a god.

NEON

Most of us tend to use neon as an adjective more than a name; it's a word we use to describe things that are of a bright, somewhat gaudy colour and light. This is because many of the things we describe as neon are made with neon lighting that uses this element to create that signature glow. Neon lighting can be found all around us, from signs behind a bar to cities like Las Vegas and Bangkok being drenched in them. Neon lights have become such a staple of our lives that they have elevated the word outside of the world of chemistry. Despite the man-made artificial image neon now has, it is first and foremost a naturally occurring element.

While a lot of elements follow certain naming conventions, neon has a unique name in the fact that there aren't any other elements that have a name similar to it. Its etymology is of interest but shows us just how little foresight people can have at times. Neon was first discovered in 1898, which is well over one hundred years ago by now but not too far back in the realm of science. Its discoverers were so excited about finding a new element that they named it after the fact that it was new, dubbing it neon. This comes from the Greek word for new, *neos*.

Since the discovery of neon, another thirty-nine elements
have been discovered. In fact, neon's discoverers William
Ramsay and Morris Travers discovered another element,
xenon, just three weeks after they discovered neon. This
means that the name neon was only accurate for less
than a month. Nevertheless, the name neon has clearly
stuck around, despite it being a complete lie. Maybe I
am a tad too pedantic; I guess it's still new in the grand
scheme of elements.

MERCURY

Mercury has the honour of being the only metallic
element that is a liquid at room temperature; this made
mercury a desirable product in ancient times when the
world was not as understood as it is today. Many in the
past felt that mercury could have been nature's own elixir
of life; they drank the stuff in hopes it would give them
everlasting life. Of course, quite the opposite happened as
most succumbed to mercury poisoning.

153

Mercury has been given quite a few names over the
years. The ancient Greeks called it *hydrargyrum,*
meaning water-silver, a fitting name for earth's most
well-known liquid metal. Over time, this element became
heavily linked with speed, perhaps due to its speed at
becoming a liquid. For whatever reason, this speed gave
it the name of quicksilver, which, like its Greek name, is
fitting too. Its speed also gave us the name mercury.
Once again, this is an element named after a god, in
this case the Roman messenger god Mercury. To deliver
messages for the gods means you have to be speedy;

thankfully, Mercury was the fastest of all the gods. It was this god's speed and the element's speed that linked these two together.

The element isn't the only thing named after this god, as the planet closest to our sun has the name Mercury too. This planet is named after the god for similar reasons as the element, as this planet orbits the sun faster than any of the other planets. That gives us a god, an element, a planet (and a superhero if we include that name of Quicksilver) that are all connected by speed.

COBALT

In ancient times, it was thought there were just seven different metals—iron, copper, tin, lead, mercury, silver, and gold. This was believed even until the sixteenth century. It was around this time that silver was being heavily mined in Germany. It was under the earth of Saxony where miners thought that they had come across huge veins of silver. They would all be rich. After extracting all this metal and putting it in the furnace to smelt, things took a turn. Instead of producing valuable silver, the ores turned into worthless lumps. They carried on trying but not only did this "silver" not smelt correctly, but many of the miners also started to fall ill due to toxic fumes they realised this metal was producing when extracted. Whatever this metal was, it definitely wasn't silver, despite how much it looked like silver in the ground.

As mentioned, people thought there were just seven metals at this time, so the thought of it being a new metal didn't enter anyone's mind. The miners came to a much more logical and realistic conclusion. They believed that this metal had been bewitched by pesky little trolls and goblins. This was a different time, you must remember, so the idea of trolls messing with metal was more likely to these people than it being a whole new metal. The theory was that trolls would create this silver-looking poisonous metal just to annoy the miners, or they would take the real silver themselves and leave behind this deadly imitator. Either way, the German miners were annoyed with these trolls. To decide what kind of trolls were toying with their metal, they looked to German folklore and the *kobold*, a pesky imp/troll from old Germanic tales. *Kobold* trolls were blamed for this tricksy metal, and their name was applied to the metal. It was only in the eighteenth century that it was decided that this wasn't some troll-tainted metal but a brand new one. Though the name had stuck by then, and eventually, it became the name cobalt as we know it today.

This element has its name thanks to the fact that it was believed trolls were trolling with the metals. If only modern trolls were that fun. It's truly crazy to know that an element on the periodic table is named after a silly little goblin. What's even crazier is that it is not the only element to be named after a goblin. The element of nickel comes from a similar origin, except it was mistaken for copper instead of silver. Originally this element was called *kupfernickel*, coming from Germanic origins, meaning copper demon. Though eventually, this name was shortened to just nickel. This means that the five-cent coin of the United States is named after these goblins too, as these coins were originally primarily made from nickel.

ARSENIC

This element has garnered sniggers from Brits, Aussies, and Irish people for some time now. Perhaps Americans would laugh at it too, if it was called assnic. Despite the name, it has nothing to do with backsides. Arsenic seems to be most linked with its historical use as a poison; however, the element does have other, less dangerous uses too. Arsenic in its natural form has a striking yellow colour to it, and it's from this colour it got its name.

Arsenic predates the concept of the periodic table and the nomenclature of modern elements, meaning its name comes from pretty ancient roots. It ultimately comes from the Persian word of *zarnikh*, meaning "yellow orpiment," with an orpiment being the proper name for the type of minerals arsenic is found in. This sounds a little like the modern word we have today. When the Greeks got their hands on this deadly stuff, they translated its name from the Persian word into their Greek name of *arsenikon*, which then the Romans turned into the Latin name of *arsenicum*.

XENON

I hinted toward this element in a previous entry. This was the element the discoverers of neon discovered three weeks after they had dubbed neon the "new" element. Of course, they had already dubbed an element as new, so they couldn't give this even newer element that name as well. Well, they had to get a little more creative this time. For this element, they drew inspiration from the Greek word of *xenos*, which means things like "foreign/strange." I imagine this was because this new element of xenon was foreign, new, and strange in the periodic table—a creative idea. Ramsay and Travers, who discovered neon and xenon, carried on being creative with their element names as they discovered more than these two. Krypton was another one of their discoveries. This one comes from the Greek word for hidden, *kryotos*. I imagine it was this alien-sounding name that inspired the name of a certain alien's home planet as well as the name of his one weakness.

THORIUM

Krypton isn't the only element to have ties to the world of superheroes and comic books, though the figure we are covering this time existed way before comic books were even a thing. The element of thorium gets its name from the realm of mythology; however, unlike the aforementioned helium that shares its name with a figure from Greek mythology, thorium comes from the myths of another part of the world, the realm of Norse mythology.

157

While there are many known gods from these stories, the mighty Thor is undoubtedly the most beloved of them all, and a certain comic/film franchise has helped cement that. Though why is this unknown element named after the hammer-wielding god of thunder? Is it incredibly strong and durable like Thor? Or is it conducive to things like lightning? Well, neither of those seem to be the case exactly. This new element was isolated via a mineral from the mining town of Falun in the nation of Sweden. This name of thorium is an ode to the nation from which it came, the Viking nation of Sweden.

EINSTEINIUM

Elements aren't only named after mythological people. They can be named after real people too; normally, when they are named after real people, those people tend to be big wigs in the world of chemistry and science in general. There are few people on our planet more closely linked with science than Albert Einstein.

I am sure you don't need me to introduce Einstein; that name alone has become synonymous with intelligence, and his look has morphed into a caricature for scientists. If anyone is going to have an element named after them, it has to be him. It was a team from the University of California–Berkeley that got the honour of naming this element when it was first identified in 1952. The team boiled it down to two contenders for whom the element should be named after, Einstein or Enrico Fermi. Of course, Einstein won out eventually, but unfortunately, between the element being identified and having his name officially bestowed upon it, the great thinker passed away. His legacy lives on in many ways, with this element being named after him just one of those ways. Don't feel too bad for Enrico Fermi, though, as the following element of fermium was named after him.

These aren't the only two elements to be named after real people. There's also curium named after Marie and Pierre Curie, nobelium named after Alfred Nobel, and mendelevium named after Dmitri Mendeleev, the man who created the periodic table.

THULIUM

Another popular way of naming elements is after places; typically, these are places that relate to the element in one way or another. Also typically, these places exist. With thulium, that isn't quite the case. I wouldn't be too shocked to hear that you have never heard of the land of Thule. It doesn't appear on any modern maps. Look at ancient Greek and Roman maps, and there's a higher chance that Thule will be on there. Thule was the name given to the northernmost island known to the ancient Mediterranean world. Some claim to have been there, while others hypothesised about its existence. What Thule was, in reality, we aren't too sure. Some have suggested it was maybe the Shetland islands off the coast of Scotland, or even the Faroe Islands even more north. Some even think it was Iceland or Greenland. All these ancient people knew for certain is that this mythical island was the farthest point in their world.

159

Thule lives on, however; it's the namesake for some ships and bases in Greenland. One of Greenland's northernmost towns is fittingly known as Thule/New Thule too. Of course, for us, it is the namesake of this element. This element was discovered by a Swedish chemist, Per Teodor Cleve. He named it thulium as an ode to his home country of Sweden. While some feel that Thule was an island of some sort, others claim that Thule was the name for ancient Scandinavia. Some say it was the land area's earliest known name. It's this supposedly ancient name for his homelands as to why he named this chemical after this ancient name.

Adjectives

Hold on a minute; those aren't names? Well, yes, that is certainly the case, but these books are called the origin of names *and* words, aren't they? So for one chapter and one chapter only, let's take a quick detour from our favourite word class of nouns and look at another word class entirely, adjectives. Adjectives are, of course, words we use to describe things. If nouns are the bread and butter of language, then adjectives are surely the spices. You could say, "the dog," but isn't it much more fun to say, "the big, silly, hairy dog"? Adjectives come from all sorts of places, as you will see in the well-known and obscure ones that I have chosen to shine a light on. Of course, the word "adjective" itself isn't an adjective but a noun. "Adjective" comes from Latin meaning "to throw toward," as these words are used in conjunction with other words; they throw toward words like nouns and such.

BIG

Big is one of the most popular adjectives in the English language. When we are first coming to grips with different classes of words, big is the adjectives many teachers and parents use as an example. This would lead you to presume that big comes from some deep Latin or even proto-Indo-European root. That isn't quite the case. In the grand scheme of words, it doesn't date too far back; some of the earliest uses of it are from the fourteenth century. It was a word primarily used in northern England. This has led many etymologists to believe that big may have arrived in the English language from Viking origins, as so much of northern England at this time was ruled by Vikings. It may have come from their word of *bugge*, meaning "great man," before going on to pillage the rest of the language in true Viking fashion.

So what word was the rest of English using to describe things of a great size before big came onto the scene? That honour supposedly goes to the Old English word of *micel*. While this exact word doesn't exist, it went on to create the adjective of much, which still has links with being big and grand. If we say something is too much, it can mean something is too big.

HERCULEAN

Sometimes, certain figures can have such a legacy and be so closely linked with one thing in particular that we use their name to describe the thing they were best known for. This is exactly the case with the mighty word of herculean. If you were to describe something as herculean, you would be saying that it was something of enormous strength or courage. It's almost as if the courage that was displayed was equal to that of Hercules himself, the Greek hero known for his tremendous strength. Hercules became so well-known for his physical prowess and his amazing bravery that anyone else shown to possess these qualities would be compared to him. This eventually gave us that adjective of herculean.

163

While Hercules may be a mythological figure, we have also created adjectives based on real people and their qualities. Take the adjective of Orwellian, made in the ode of George Orwell, to describe anything similar to a dystopian surveillance state. We also have Dickensian, named after Charles Dickens, used to describe the image of Victorian London and England as a whole in the way Dickens did best. In fact, Victorian is another prime example, coming from the name of Queen Victoria to describe her time on the throne. A personal favourite of mine has to be Pythonesque, a word coined thanks to the comedy group of Monty Python, a word used to describe anything surreal, funny, bizarre, and downright silly.

ABYSMAL

If something were to be described as abysmal, it would not be a good thing; it would be something worse than pathetic, worse than miserable, worse than hopeless. Abysmal should be used when there is no metaphorical ray of light to help brighten a situation. When the word abysmal first came around in the seventeenth century, it referred to somewhere where literal light could not shine. Abysmal was initially an adjective used to describe something pertaining to an abyss—a deep, dark void. For example, if for some reason you had a house in an abyss, you could describe it as being an abysmal house.

An abyss is a miserable, hopeless place. If you found yourself in an abyss, you probably aren't in the best of places, metaphorically or literally. Thanks to this, the word abysmal started to take on a more metaphorical meaning when it started being used to describe something extremely bad or awful. As for where abyss itself came from, it is thought to come from the Greek *byssos*, meaning bottom, with A at the start being a popular word-forming prefix meaning without. *Abyssos*

would mean without bottom, as many abysses are described as never-ending. Even in a section all about adjectives, I am finding ways to explain nouns.

CLUMSY

This feels like an adjective I am all too familiar with, and my fellow clumsy people are too. It's interesting that clumsy is now linked with flailing around but to start it was quite the opposite. Clumsy began its life by meaning to be numb and stiff. It meant to be numb for a specific reason. Clumsy comes from the Middle English word of *clumsid*, meaning to be numb with cold, a feeling I am sure a lot of us are familiar with during cold winter months. Over time, this word of *clumsid* became clumsy and took its modern meaning, used to describe the less dexterous among us. What I love most about this etymology is that clumsy is a blending of the words of cold and numb, which is wonderfully fitting.

165

HUMDRUM

Humdrum is a word many people don't want to be linked with; it is defined as something dull, monotonous, and boring. There are definitely worse words someone could be called. Personally, I think humdrum is a cute word. The word is believed to have more to do with humming than drumming. Humming is, of course, when we make a tune in our mouths, as well as being a word we use to describe any sort of buzzing sound. Whether we are making a humming sound or if something else is making a humming sound, the implication is the same. Humming is closely linked with being boring or dull. Humming is something we do when we are doing dull routines, and the monotonous hum of a bug or piece of tech is irksome too. Hum is a word that ties with being boring.

Drums, on the other hand, are far from boring or dull, so why have they been thrown into this adjective too? Well, the drum in humdrum came about simply from reduplication. Reduplicating words or sounds is something we humans love to do. Children are well-known for creating words out of reduplication, like with mama and dada. However, we grown-ups do it too. Often, the exact word isn't replicated, but a similar-sounding word is—think of things like yoo-hoo, hip-hop, and pitter-patter. Humdrum is just believed to be some fun reduplication to spice an otherwise humdrum word.

LETHARGIC

Have you ever felt beyond lazy? So lazy that you can't even be bothered to... You know, I couldn't even be bothered to finish that sentence. When you are feeling this level of unproductiveness, the word lazy might not even cut just how meh you are feeling. Instead, why not use the word lethargic, meaning feeling lazy? Lethargic can mean other things too, like being incredibly tired or just sluggish after a big meal.

Many adjectives are formed from nouns; think of hairy to describe someone with a lot of hair. Lethargic is another instance of this. However, its root noun isn't as popular as the word hair. Lethargic comes from lethargy, a noun we use when excitement is limited (for example, reading this book left me with a great sense of lethargy). To understand this adjective, we have to understand this noun. Lethargy comes from the Greek *lēthargos*, which is a combination of Greek words meaning "forgetful and idle." These two words greatly sum up what lethargy is, feeling idle and forgetful.

BIONIC

The word-forming element of bio is one we heavily link with all things living and the natural world. It literally comes from the Greek word for life, and we see it in words like biology, the study of living organisms. Yet, the adjective of bionic doesn't describe something that is alive and natural; in fact, it describes quite the opposite. We use bionic to describe things that are "artificial, electronic, and mechanical." If someone told you they had a bionic leg, then you may picture a robotic leg in your mind, not a flesh-and-bone leg. Why do we use a word so heavily linked with organic life to describe something so robotic?

167

Well, bionic isn't a word we use for everything that relates to the word of technology. You wouldn't describe a laptop or mobile phone as bionic. We tend to use bionic when we are describing something that is a mix of technological and organic, like the aforementioned bionic leg. Even something completely technological we could call bionic, like a bionic dog. Even though a bionic dog may be completely robotic, it's still based on the real animal. Bionic is used when the biological world and the electronic world are blended together, and it's from this blend where the word bionic comes from. Bionic is simply a blending of the word bio with the last three letters of the word electronic, as something that is bionic is both biological and electronic. Bionic, in this sense, was first recorded in 1963 and rose to fame with fictional characters like the Six Million Dollar Man, the Terminator, Inspector Gadget, and Robocop.

While we relate bionic most with modern popular culture, the word dates back to the start of the twentieth century. Bionic, in this sense, was an adjective not being used by nerds and geeks but instead by paleontologists, who probably were geeky but a different kind of geeky. In the world of fossils, bionic was used to describe organisms that could successfully repeat certain characteristics over generations.

ABSTRACT

It's hard to picture in your mind something that could be described as abstract, as today abstract means something along the lines of that. Something that has no real concrete image or idea is described as abstract; it can even mean bizarre. Abstract has perhaps found itself best at home in the realm of art. Before abstract had such an ephemeral meaning, it meant something more simple to grasp. Abstract was used to describe something drawn away, perhaps in a literal sense with pulling a cart away. Or maybe in a metaphorical sense, meaning someone who is reclusive.

Abstract itself starts with the word-forming element of ab, which means "away from"; we see it in other words like abnormal and abduction. The -stract part of the name comes from the Latin *trahere*, meaning to "draw/drag." So abstract has a literal etymology, in spite of how we use this word to describe un-literal things. It's easy to see how this word describes the action of dragging things away back to describe things that have been dragged away from our reality.

NICE

Nice is a word we use to describe good, kind, generous people. By and large, it is a positive word. Nice isn't a word we would brand with someone we don't like. Once upon a time, that was the case; despite its modern meaning, nice does not have the nicest of etymologies. Before we had nice, we had the Latin *nescius*, which meant things like "ignorant" or "foolish." This Latin word came from the Latin elements of *ne* and *scire*, meaning "not" and "to know," respectively. So this Latin word meant "not too known." This wasn't the kindest of adjectives to use for people.

169

How did this word we would use to describe dumb people come to be used to describe kind people? Well, that shift started in the fourteenth century. By now, the word had become nice as we spell it today; however, its meaning hadn't fully changed yet. In this century, nice was used to describe excessively luxurious things. How it made this shift, I am not too sure. As the years went on, this luxurious meaning began to soften. By the fifteenth

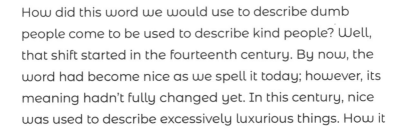

century, nice would be used to describe things that were refined and cultured. And being refined like this was seen as a good, kind way of living by the eighteenth century; the word nice got applied to these refined, kind people. Eventually, it was applied to all kind people, regardless of their wealth and lifestyle. You may be wondering if the city in France has anything to do with this adjective; that doesn't seem to be the case. Nice in France comes from the Greek word for victory, *nikaios,* hence why the city's name sounds somewhat similar to the name of the Greek goddess of victory, Nike, who went on to be the namesake of a shoe brand.

▬
MELANCHOLY
▬

Despite devoting my life to names and all things nouns, you may be surprised to hear that my favourite word in the English language is an adjective, with that being this adjective, melancholy. Melancholy is a word used to describe that feeling of sadness you may get for no obvious reason. Sure, it's not the funniest word, and having it as my favourite might make me seem like a downer. But there's something I enjoy so much about it. It's okay to feel sad at times, even when we don't know why exactly.

If melancholy's definition didn't put you off the word, then its etymology certainly will. For those morbidly curious, carry on reading. Melancholy comes from the Greek *melankholia,* which means "sadness" and "excess of black bile," which is pretty gross. It breaks down to the Greek *melas,* meaning "black," and *khole,* meaning "bile." I think it'd be pretty glum if I had way too much black bile. While black bile unto itself sounds pretty unappealing, what exactly does this mean? Well, the idea of black bile goes back to ancient Greece when we didn't fully understand how the human body worked. To summarise, many philosophers and physicians thought that the human body was run by four different fluids known as the humours. These controlled our well-being and emotions. These four fluids are/were blood, phlegm, yellow bile, and black bile. Black bile was believed to be produced by the spleen, and having an overload of it in your body made you feel sad, among other things. Of course, this idea of anatomy isn't quite the case. Though, this gross concept over excess black bile gave us the pretty word of melancholy.

Last Names

We started this book with first names, so it only seems fitting to wrap things up with last names. These sorts of names go by a variety of names: last names, family names, surnames. Whatever you call them, these are the names that some hold more value in, as they are the ones more traditionally carried through a family. Thanks to this tradition, these names have the ability to outlast the majority of family members who hold them. This does not mean that every family has a unique last name. Some last names appear more than others. There are also different last names from around the globe. I am going to be looking at a selection of these names from more to less popular ones, from all the corners of the globe. One last thing I ought to mention about these kinds of names, despite the fact I am calling them last names, they don't always appear at the end of someone's name in every tradition.

SMITH

173

The most popular and perhaps definitive last name of the English-speaking world. If you were to ask someone to think of a surname, it's most likely they would say Smith. As we progress through this chapter, you will realise that most surnames in English come from one of a few origins, one of those being the professions of our ancestors. For example, someone with the surname Farmer probably came from a family of farmers, same for a surname like Baker. It's from occupational roots as to where we get that surname of Smith.

Someone with the surname of Smith most likely has an ancestor who was a blacksmith, people who worked with steel and iron to create things like swords and armour. The fact that there are so many people with the surname Smith still around today implies that there must have been an awful lot of blacksmiths grafting away in the past. However, not everyone in the past needed a sword nor had the money to afford a fancy suit of armour, so why has Smith become such a popular last name if being a blacksmith wasn't the most popular line of work? Well, a blacksmith was just one kind of smith, despite being the most popular. There were also goldsmiths who worked with gold, coppersmiths who worked with copper, bladesmiths who made weapons, whitesmiths who worked with tin, and even green smiths who worked with lead. All these kinds of smiths were working away, using their occupation as a last name; over the years, however, most of these got shortened down to just Smith. Some of these full smith titles do live on as last names, the best example being Goldsmith, a last name that is still somewhat popular, though not as commonplace as Smith.

This opens up one more question: why were these metal workers called smiths in the first place? Well, it's believed that this occupational name of smith relates to the verb "smite," meaning "to strike something with tremendous power." Metalsmiths do an awful lot of smiting to metal, and over time smite evolved into smith.

FORD

Another popular way in which last names came into being was with people of the past taking on names that reflected where they lived. Sometimes, this was more specific to a town or any kind of settlement, like the last name of Lincoln, ultimately deriving from the city of Lincoln in the UK. Sometimes, these surnames were vaguer, and instead of pointing to a specific town or city, they referred to a geographic feature. This appears to be the case with the popular surname of Ford.

Fords definitely aren't the most well-known of geographic features. When you imagine last names that derive from geographic features, I imagine the likes of woods or hills may come to mind. A ford is just as much a part of our natural world as these things, with a ford being a specific part of a river where the river gets exceptionally shallow, so shallow that we, our animals, and our wheels are able to cross safely. It would have been those who lived next to these watery crossings that adopted their name as their own. The word ford unto itself is ancient and ultimately comes from the proto-Indo-European *prtu,* meaning "a passage." It's also from this PIE word where we go port and harbour from.

175

A notable Ford is, of course, Henry Ford, the creator of Ford cars. Ford also became a verb meaning "to cross a ford." I mention these things as they allow this sentence to be grammatically correct: Ford's Ford fords fords. I'll let you figure out for yourself what this means.

KENNEDY

As a last name of Irish Celtic origins, you may presume Kennedy has some beautiful Irish meaning, but that isn't the case. Many surnames come from characteristics the original holders had, whether physical characteristics like the surnames of Short or personality characteristics like the surname of Wise. Kennedy is a last name coming from a physical characteristic, and it is not the most flattering either.

Kennedy is believed to be the anglicized form of the Irish surname Ceannéidigh, believed to come from the Gaelic words of *ceann* and éidigh, which mean ugly and head, respectively. So the original bearer of this name must not have had the prettiest face. It's far from the most flattering of names! Not all hope is lost, as some claim that it doesn't mean ugly head, but instead means "fierce head." So maybe the original Kennedy had a terrifying face that scared all the other tribes away. Other theories point to it meaning helmet head or even helmeted chief. My personal favourite has to be the ugly head meaning.

176

HOROWITZ

Many last names are proudly Jewish, with Horowitz being a prime example of a Jewish surname. Many of these Jewish surnames come from Slavic origins and have found their way across the globe via the many Jewish diasporas that have happened over the course of history. The last name of Horowitz has now made itself at home in nations like the UK and USA; however, it has roots in the historical region of Bohemia, which is now firmly part of the modern Slavic nation of Czechia. Horowitz is another location-based last name, pointing to a specific town, Hořovice in Czechia. This town had one of the largest Jewish populations in the entire Kingdom of Bohemia while it existed. This explains why this settlement became the basis of such a popular Jewish surname.

The -witz part at the end of this name is found in countless Slavic and Jewish surnames. It simply means "son of/child of." So it seems kind of out of place being attached to a town name. As far as I am aware, this town never parented any children. I guess people with this last name were children of Hořovice in a more metaphorical sense than a biological sense. Perhaps by the time this last name came into being, it was such a normal convention to end last names with -witz that they did it to every last name regardless of what the first part meant.

GUERRERO

We touched upon occupation-based surnames with Smith, and Guerrero is another one of those of Spanish origin. However, the occupation it relates to isn't quite as mundane as farmer or baker. The Spanish word for war is *guerra,* and war is where this surname comes from. I have read that this surname means a variety of things, all relating to combat in some way. Some sources say it means "fighter," while others specify it means "soldier" or even "warrior." While this is a name of Spanish origin, it has spread across the Atlantic because of Spanish rule in South America. Thanks to this, the surname of

Guerrero has found even more popularity in Mexico than in its native Spain. Perhaps it's so popular due to the many wars Mexico has played a role in, with the most noticeable being their own war for independence. One of the generals in this revolution and the nation's second president had this last name, Vicente Guerrero. It's undoubtedly a fitting last name for someone so heavily linked to war.

KNICKERBOCKER

Knickerbocker is, without doubt, one of the funnest last names to say. It's an incredibly unique one too. It's a name of Dutch roots but not thought to have been created in The Netherlands. Instead, it's thought to have been a last name created by Dutch settlers in the city of New Amsterdam. New Amsterdam would, of course, go under a name change, becoming New York City. It's in the city that never sleeps where the name of Knickerbocker still holds some cultural resonance.

178

Knickerbocker itself became a term for New Yorkers. I read it was used for all from Manhattan, the Dutch settlers of the city, and even the upper crust of society there. Either way, those from NYC don't call themselves Knickerbockers all too much these days. It became so closely linked with New York thanks to the book *A History of New York* written by dutchman Diedrich Knickerbocker, who was famous author Washington Irving under a false Dutch name. It was also thanks to this book that many people saw drawings of traditional Dutch pants, which got the name Knickerbocker attached to them too. This got shortened into just knickers and is still used today, primarily in England, as the name for underwear traditionally worn by women. There's, of course, the Knickerbocker Glory too, a beloved sundae that supposedly has its roots in the Big Apple.

Knickerbocker is a word that has gotten around, despite how rarely it is seen as a last name today. What does it mean? Well, it's believed to have been a Dutch word created in America. The first part of the name is thought to come from the Dutch *knikker*, meaning "marble," and the Dutch *bakker*, meaning "baker." So the name means "marble baker." Baking marbles might seem like a strange concept, but it relates to the glass sphere marbles as opposed to the type of rock marble. When you bake toy marbles, they become all cracked and pretty.

WANG

With a recorded 100 million Wangs in China alone, Wang holds the title of not just the most popular last name in mainland China but also as one of the most popular last names worldwide. While I am calling this a last name, that isn't the case with this one, as traditionally, in Chinese names, the family name goes first. For example, the ancient Chinese emperor Wang Mang would have been given the name of Mang, with Wang being his family name that was passed on; we can see this clearly with his children who were called Wang Yu, Wang Huo, and Wang An, just to name three of them.

Wang Mang is a good example of a Wang, as the "last" name of Wang means exactly what he was, "king." Yep, the name of Wang simply means "king" in Chinese. I guess people would have taken on this name in honour of their ruler, as I don't think all the Chinese people with the name to this day are descendants of a king. While this might seem strange at first, you must remember that king unto itself is a popular last name in English too. A certain horror writer comes to mind.

KHAN

This is a South Asian last name with a deep history. Before being a last name at all, it was a title, simply meaning ruler or chief in various Asian languages. Originally, it was *khagan* in the fourth century before being shortened to just Khan. To start with, Khans would have just been rulers or chiefs of small communities. The power of one Khan spread far and wide; as he spread his power, he also spread his name too. With his name being...Temüjin?

180

That probably wasn't quite the name you were expecting, and that's because Temüjin was the name that a certain Genghis Khan was born with. Though as his mighty Mongol Empire grew larger and covered more land, he quickly adopted a new name for himself. He obviously took on the title of Khan for himself; it would have been a word he was familiar with and after all, he was a ruler. He was way more than a ruler of a small town or community. His title had to be grander. That's why he added Genghis before Khan, which is believed to mean either universal or oceanic. This is because the land he ruled was so large it went from ocean to ocean, and in their time, it would have seemed like he conquered the known universe. While Genghis Khan was just a chosen title, he became so known by it that many thought it was just his name.

It fits our usual naming conventions; it's easy to see why Genghis became a first name and Khan a last. While Khan most likely would have become a last name anyway, Genghis' domination of Eurasian helped cement its fate. In fact, it might be more than his name that lives on today, as some studies suggest that one in every two hundred men alive today are a descendant of Genghis Khan, meaning Khan has become an inherited name and not just a title given to a select few.

CHRISTODOULOPOULOS

Greek surnames often have a wonderful sound to them, and Christodoulopoulos is no exception. Despite how alien this name might seem at first to non-native speakers, once you break it down, it's a lot easier to understand. Let's start with the back end of this name first. *Opoulos* is a common element in Greek surnames, and it means "descendant of." Looking at the first part of this name might lead you to believe this name means "descendant of Christopher," and while that may be the case for some, you must remember that Greece is a Christian country.

181

While it's a debated subject, Jesus himself isn't thought to have had any children, so having this name does not directly imply that Jesus Christ is your great-great-great-great-great-grandfather or anything like that. Instead, it's believed to mean you are a descendant of something who worshipped Jesus, maybe even a priest or something. So this name is kind of a two-in-one. Not only is it a family-based last name but also possibly an occupation-based one.

-son

One of the most common ways you will see last names ending in the English language are with the three little letters of "son." This is pretty easy to understand. It simply means son of and has Viking roots. In Iceland to this day, most boys get "son" attached to their last names. While daughters get "dottir." In the wider English-speaking world, however, both men and women can be called son. The first part of these son last names usually implies whose son you are. This is extremely easy to tell in some names, like the last names of Johnson and Peterson. We can clearly see the names of John and Peter in these names.

Other first names don't mesh as nicely with the -son suffix, so more letters have to be applied for grammatical reasons. Patrickson doesn't sound too good, so it was adapted into Patterson. The same goes for Andrewson becoming Anderson and Jefferyson becoming Jefferson. However, the start of some of these son last names sounds nothing like the first names we have today. Take Hudson for example. Hud isn't a first name I have come across. It's believed that the Hud in Hudson comes from the medieval name of Hudde, believed to be the pet form of either Huge (which sounds similar) or Richard (which does not sound similar). Then we have Dawson too, which relates to the name David. Davidson unto itself is a popular last name, so how we ended up with Dawson and Davidson, I'm not too sure. Perhaps there were so many people called David that to help tell their ancestors apart that these two different last names were created.

Some of these "son" last names don't relate to a first name at all. For example, we have Bronson, which simply means the son of someone with brown hair. I guess those original Bronsons didn't care for their parents enough to use their name but enjoyed their hair colour. With the influx of people creating new unique first names for their children today, perhaps these will go on to create some new son-inspired last names that will be with us in the future.

What Comes Next?

That, for now, wraps up another exciting etymological adventure. I set out for this book to be a deeper dive into the world of word origins, more off the beaten path than the subjects covered in the first book. Instead of playing it safe with the likes of counties and cities, we plunged into watery words and historical places. Finally, looking into the first and last names of humans put our feet safely back on solid ground. There's one question I find myself asking, however: what comes next?

We have proven again with this book that so many of the words and names around us have deep, interesting origins. While we might be coming up for air now, I already want to dive deeper. I want to look into other subjects and topic areas, find odd and popular words and names within those, and once again ask myself that question I seem to constantly be asking, "How did it get its name?"

Maybe I am getting too ahead of myself. Let's take a break and enjoy the facts we have found out in this book, shall we? Remember, please don't keep these facts to yourself; share them with the world. Tell your friends, family, colleagues, and classmates. I hope these books give you the same excitement for etymology that I have. Perhaps now you may feel prepared to go on your own etymological adventures!

185

Bye for Now

If you are in any way interested in exploring the world of etymology for yourself, that is great! I want to give this gift to all of you, like Prometheus stealing fire from the gods to give to the humans. Hopefully, the word gods won't tie me to a rock and send an eagle to eat my liver. Before I wrap up this book, I want to highlight some terrific sources and other books that not only helped with the research for this book but can help you research how words came to be for yourself.

ONLINE RESOURCES

Thanks to the world wide web, most questions are a mere search engine away, so much so, in fact, sometimes I feel more inclined to call myself a professional Googler as opposed to a YouTuber or author. While many sites come up, there are a few I'd recommend. Poor old Wikipedia gets a bad rap, and while its ability to be edited by anyone can be seen as a bad thing, it's a great thing too. The world's collective knowledge, powered by those who know best, all in one place. Just make sure to check the sources if anything seems iffy to you.

187

The Online Etymology Dictionary (etymonline) is a fantastic website containing the origins of many words. Plus, it's all sourced, making me feel confident in using it and recommending it. While it exists in a collection of huge books, the Oxford English Dictionary's website is my go-to dictionary. It's easy to use, gives clear definitions, examples, historical uses of words, and even brief etymologies. While it isn't free, you can access it for free via a library membership in most cases. It's likely your school or institute already has an account you can use, and if they don't, pester them until they do!

Recently, I have been looking into the names we use for ourselves, and two websites have been of extreme use. NameBerry is a terrific, easy-to-use site with tons of name origins and meanings. It's definitely geared toward expecting parents, so as well as finding out names' meanings, it may tell you if it's hot or not at the moment. Behind the Name is another great name website too. It's dryer than NameBerry but doesn't have an expected-parent angle, just the facts. Behind the Name highlights other things like how names have been interpreted around the globe. If it were not for Behind the Name, I would never know that the name Guillermo is just the Spanish interpretation of William. Who'd have thought?

BOOKS

You can't beat a good book. Despite being an author, I admit I find it hard to sit and read at times. Recently, however, a switch has flicked in my brain, and now I can't seem to put books down! To recommend just a handful of books is difficult, but I have narrowed it down to five for now. Bill Bryson and David Crystal are, in my eyes, some of the highest authorities on the English language. Not only do they know their stuff, but they write in an engaging way I can only hope to achieve. Bryson's book *Mother Tongue* and Crystal's *A Little Book of Language* are great places to start your quest on understanding the quagmire of English.

If you want to focus on etymologies as opposed to language in general, then a great place to start is with Mark Forsyth's *The Etymologicon*, one of the most popular books on etymology out there and it's perfectly written. One word blends into another seamlessly. Go read it. If you are from the UK and into words, then you have undoubtedly heard of Susie Dent, the authority on words in "dictionary corner" on the quiz show *Countdown*. Her recently released book *Word Perfect* is a terrific read. It's broken down into days of the year with an etymology for each day. If you aren't an avid reader and can only manage a small bit each day, then this book is written with that goal in mind.

Finally, Neil Burdess' great read *Hello, My Name Is* has to be one of the best books on first and last names out there. It must be the only book focused on names that doesn't feature the word "baby" anywhere in its title. If you want a complete understanding of first and last names in English, this is the book for you.

189

WRITING ALL ALONE

By the time you are reading these words, I sincerely hope the world is in a much better place. This entire book has been written in the midst of the COVID-19 pandemic that has brought much of the world to a halt. It's not something I wanted to highlight by any means, but I felt strange if I didn't mention it. My line of work and life has fortunately been largely unaffected by things, though my days of typing away in coffee shops watching the world go by are sorely missed. My thoughts go out to everyone who has suffered at the hands of this terrible virus. I can only hope my work has been something of a distraction from the wider world in these trying times. Of course, a huge thank you has to be given to those who have played vital, key roles in the midst of this pandemic, from shop-floor assistants to those working in hospitals. You have kept this crazy world spinning in this crazy time. Let's hope that this single paragraph becomes a time capsule of sorts for a piece of history that will soon be behind us.

THANK YOU

When I wrote my first book, I never thought anyone would want a second. So I put all my thank yous and love into the end of that first one. Don't I feel silly being in this position again. I shan't gush with affection this time around as much as I did last time, but a huge thank you has to be given to everyone in my life who has supported me in the writing of this book and in my everyday life. Thank you to my family, partner, friends, fellow creators, all those behind the scenes at Mango, and of course, you guys who read these books and watch my videos. *Name Explain* would not exist online or on these pages if it were not for the support you have all shown me along the way. That was still too mushy, wasn't it? I'll try and be even blunter next time.

About the Author

Patrick Foote is the creator of the YouTube channel *Name Explain*, which for over five years has covered the etymologies and origins of hundreds of different names, words, countries, people, animals, and so much more. He was born in London and lives in the Soutwest of England. *Name Explain* came into being from Patrick's love of language and his drive to find answers for questions that lingered in his brain. Through his work on YouTube, Patrick started writing books on his beloved topic of etymology. His first title *The Origin of Names, Words, and Everything in Between* went on to become a number one bestseller across the globe. When Patrick isn't explaining names, he is usually playing video games, watching professional wrestling, building LEGO sets, or tending to his pet tortoise Bowser.

Mango Publishing, established in 2014, publishes an eclectic list of books by diverse authors—both new and established voices—on topics ranging from business, personal growth, women's empowerment, LGBTQ studies, health, and spirituality to history, popular culture, time management, decluttering, lifestyle, mental wellness, aging, and sustainable living. We were recently named 2019 *and* 2020's #1 fastest growing independent publisher by *Publishers Weekly*. Our success is driven by our main goal, which is to publish high quality books that will entertain readers as well as make a positive difference in their lives.

Our readers are our most important resource; we value your input, suggestions, and ideas. We'd love to hear from you—after all, we are publishing books for you!

Please stay in touch with us and follow us at:

Facebook: Mango Publishing
Twitter: @MangoPublishing
Instagram: @MangoPublishing
LinkedIn: Mango Publishing
Pinterest: Mango Publishing
Newsletter: mangopublishinggroup.com/newsletter

Join us on Mango's journey to reinvent publishing, one book at a time.